FOUR STEPS TO SPIRITUAL FREEDOM

Thomas Ryan

Paulist Press
New York/Mahwah, N.J.

Unless otherwise noted, scripture quotations are from the New Revised Standard Version of the Bible, copyright 1989 by the Division of Christian Education of the National Council of Churches of Christ in the U.S.A.

Prayers used in the last chapter are from *Hearts on Fire: Praying with Jesuits*, Michael Harter, S.J., ed. (St. Louis: Institute of Jesuit Sources, 1993), and *The Flowering of the Soul: A Book of Prayers by Women*, Lucinda Vardley, ed. (Toronto: Alfred A. Knopf, 1999).

Book design by Lynn Else
Cover design by John Candell

Copyright © 2003 by Paulist Press, Inc.

All rights reserved. No part of this book may be reproduced or transmitted in any form or by any means, electronic or mechanical, including photocopying, recording, or by any information storage and retrieval system without permission in writing from the Publisher.

Library of Congress Cataloging-in-Publication Data

Ryan, Thomas, Father.
    Four steps to spiritual freedom / Thomas Ryan.
    ISBN 0-8091-4145-0 (alk. paper)
    1. Spiritual life—Catholic Church. 2. Liberty—Religious aspects—Catholic Church. I. Title.
    BX2350.3 .R93 2003
    248.4′82—dc21

                                              2003000732

Published by Paulist Press
997 Macarthur Boulevard
Mahwah, New Jersey 07430

www.paulistpress.com

Printed and bound in the United States of America

Acknowledgments

Special thanks to my editors: Kathleen Walsh, for helping me shape the material and hold the focus, and Father Larry Boadt, C.S.P., for his guidance in the final stage and assistance in bringing the book into port. I am grateful as well to Ann Herbert for her digitalized execution of my diagrams, and to all those who have contributed to this book by telling their stories and bringing these themes to real life.

Dedication

To John Govan, S.J., my director in the Spiritual Exercises, and to Maria Teresa Porcile, who shared something from the last chapter of her story in these pages and who now knows the lasting freedom of life on "the other side."

Contents

Other books by the author:

Fasting Rediscovered:
A Guide to Health and Wholeness for Your Body-Spirit
(out of print)

Tales of Christian Unity:
The Adventures of an Ecumenical Pilgrim
(out of print)

Wellness, Spirituality and Sports
(out of print)

A Survival Guide for Ecumenically-Minded Christians
(not Paulist Press)

Disciplines for Christian Living: Interfaith Perspectives
(Paulist Press)

Prayer of Heart and Body:
Meditation and Yoga as Christian Spiritual Practice
(Paulist Press)

1
Spiritual Freedom

Blessed be the Lord, the God of Israel; *(what?)*
he has come to his people and set them *free*....
This was the oath he swore to our father Abraham:
to set us *free* from the hands of our enemies, *(which?)*
free to worship him without fear,
holy and righteous in his sight,
all the days of our lives.
You, my child, shall be called the prophet of the Most High; *(who?)*
for you will go before the Lord to prepare his way,
to give his people knowledge of salvation
by the forgiveness of their sins.
In the tender compassion of our God
the dawn from on high shall break upon us,
to shine on those who dwell in darkness
and the shadow of death,
and to guide our feet into the way of peace
(Luke 1: 68, 73-75,77–79 NAB)

Spiritual freedom is not a "thing" that can be obtained and then hung on to. It is an inner condition of the spirit that requires continual cultivation and retuning.

As the millennium ended, I made a guided, forty-day retreat following the Spiritual Exercises of St. Ignatius of Loyola.[1] Spiritual freedom is the golden grail of the Exercises. According to John J. English in his classic work on the Spiritual Exercises, attainment of this spiritual freedom is, to a degree, the purpose of the Exercises as a whole and one of the fundamental graces of them. They are intended to serve as an instrument for bringing a person to a realized, existential freedom. The matrix out of which it flows is a deep awareness of and concordance with the ultimate meaning of one's life.

This spiritual freedom requires an acceptance of oneself as historically coming from God, going to God, and being with God. It is marked by a sense of well-being, self-identity, and inner serenity. "Who am I?" "What is my calling?" and "Where is it leading?" are questions that the spiritually free person can answer peacefully. This is not just freedom *from*; Ignatius's purpose was not to get us to leave things behind, but to discover the person of Jesus Christ and to become so consumed with love for him that we are moved to commitment, and to discover in that commitment a new freedom.[2]

In the first week of the Exercises, one meditates on who one is as a creature, sinner, and child of God. In the second week, the focus shifts to obedience to God, as exemplified in Jesus' calling and ministry; it is the occasion to ask oneself: what is *my* calling, and how fully am I living it? In the third week, the meditations center on the passion of Christ, a series of events offering a long look at passionate detachment in action. In the fourth week, the resurrection is at center stage, and one sees what comes of total dedication and obedience to God.

The foci of these four weeks provide four steps to spiritual freedom: having a realistic sense of who you are; living your calling to the full (which implies obedience to God); freedom from inordinate attachments to results; and daily entrusting your life to God, rededicating it whether in times of great consolation or excruciating difficulty.[3]

A realistic sense of who you are means having a conception of yourself as creature, sinner, and child of God, and a grounded-in-reality perception of your gifts, values, and convictions; in other words, a healthy ego. Living your calling to the full in obedience to God means that your ego is aligned with your deepest and truest self, the habitat of God, and makes its decisions and orients its life in the world out of that center. Freedom from inordinate attachments means operational freedom from the false self's craving for riches (security), honor (esteem), and power (control). Daily rededicating your life and all your efforts to God means living in the spirit of Ignatius's prayer: "Take, Lord, receive, all I have and possess. You have given all to me, now I return it." To get a better grasp of what such freedom is, looks like, and feels like, we will briefly consider each one of these constitutive components of spiritual freedom as they appear in the life of Jesus.

A Realistic Sense of Who You Are

When one has a good sense of who one is, it usually translates into authenticity and truthfulness in one's relationships. Your ease with yourself enables you to be at ease with others as well. Your acceptance of yourself with your strengths and weaknesses makes it possible for you to compassionately accept others in theirs. This awareness is not just limited to the space you occupy on the planet. It expands outward to encompass the environment and others in it. This makes for a person who is tuned-in and very alive.

Look, for example, at the figure of Jesus that emerges in the gospels. Here is a person who is astonishingly aware and responsive, immensely alive to the truth of others, and surprisingly authentic in his relationships. The scribes and Pharisees in the Temple, the Samaritan woman at the well, and the host who was inwardly criticizing him for allowing an uninvited guest to wash his feet with her hair, found that out: "Simon, I have something to say to you" (Luke 7:40 ff.).

When his disciples shared their memories of his aliveness, they must have mentioned things like his natural poet's eye, which saw significance in a cage of captive sparrows, a patch on an old wineskin, the cups and plates in a washing bowl, and the dough in a kneading trough. They must have noted how his was a practical as well as a lyrical interest, how sharp he was on organizational details like attending to the leftovers after an outdoor meal, making arrangements to have an ass ready for the ride into Jerusalem, and foreseeing a room reservation for a special meal with his closest colleagues.[4]

Jesus' sense of himself and his calling contributed to his being disconcertingly free—from family ties, from property, from the burdensome application of the laws of his religion (when hungry he took grain from the field to eat on the Sabbath, healed people on the Sabbath, and did not strictly observe ritual acts of washing before meals). Already at twelve years of age he felt no qualms about letting his parents leave the Passover celebration in Jerusalem to return to Nazareth without telling them he intended to stay on for a while to follow an inner, higher call. "'Child, why have you treated us like this? Look, your father and

I have been searching for you (for three days) in great anxiety.'
He said to them, 'Why were you searching for me? Did you not
know that I must be in my Father's house?'"(Luke 2:48, 49). All
the gospel traditions contain some reflection of the distance he
kept, even from his mother.

> Then his mother and his brothers came; and standing out-
> side, they sent to him and called him. A crowd was sitting
> around him; and they said to him, "Your mother and your
> brothers and sisters are outside, asking for you." And he
> replied, "Who are my mother and my brothers?" And look-
> ing at those who sat around him, he said, "Here are my
> mother and my brothers! Whoever does the will of God is
> my brother and sister and mother." (Mark 3:31–35)[5]

He could borrow somebody else's boat or donkey when he
needed it; he apparently felt knocking on a neighbor's door
for bread in the middle of the night was permissible; and he
could enjoy himself at a party to the point that others thought it
reprehensible.[6]

The gospels clearly portray him as someone with a strong sense
of personal autonomy, someone with a sense of who he was and
what he wanted to accomplish in life. Even when misunderstood
by his own family ("…they went out to restrain him, for people
were saying 'He has gone out of his mind'" [Mark 3:21]) and
ridiculed by the religious establishment, his clear sense of identity and purpose enabled him to stay on line with his goals. The
Gospel of John tells us that "many of his disciples turned back
and no longer went about with him" (John 6:66) due to the content of his teaching. Though slowed by defections and disbelief,

he stood his ground firmly and held on to his convictions without flinching in the face of persistent and frequently hostile opposition.[7] His own sense of himself was a compass that enabled him to stay on course even in stormy seas.

People who are spiritually free are tantalizingly alive. They take bold initiatives, do interesting things, have a taste for adventure, are not threatened by other strong personalities, can hold fast to their convictions even in the face of criticism and disapproval. The word that most adequately sums up the impact of Jesus upon his contemporaries is "alive!" In the earliest preaching of the apostles he is referred to as "the Pioneer of life," or he "who has led the way to life" (Acts 3:15). The most theologically mature pronouncement about him in the whole New Testament is "in him was life" (John 1:4). The message his disciples preached in the postresurrection period—"He is alive!"—was in utter continuity with their experience of him in the preresurrection period: They looked back and saw that "alive" was indeed what he had always been.[8]

Through all these expressions—his astonishing awareness of and responsiveness to other people, his surprising authenticity in relationships, his courageous perseverance in teaching and preaching even in the face of opposition—the image comes through clearly of a man who had a realistic sense of who he was and what he was called to do.

Live Your Calling to the Full

The second component in spiritual freedom is living one's calling to the full in obedience to God. *Obedience,* which comes from the Latin word meaning "to listen," involves prayerfully attuning ourselves to the voice of God in the many ways that God speaks to us: through our relationships, the scriptures, our consciences, church teaching and preaching, films, music, art, the books we read, the natural world. Everything in existence is part of God's vocabulary and is capable of speaking to us a word of revelation about ourselves, our world, and the meaning of our lives. In brief, Christian obedience amounts to listening sensitively for the word of God speaking in our experience, and following what we hear in loving trust. We often have to act without a guarantee that we are in fact following the will of God, but even the desire to open our lives to God's guiding influence will inevitably draw us closer to God.[9]

We have considered how alive Jesus was in his sense of himself, but most of all those who knew him well must have experienced him as a man *totally alive to God*. It was a transparent relationship of passionate intimacy and devotion from which naturally flowed the child's word "Abba" when he prayed. "I know him; if I would say that I do not know him, I would be a liar like you" (John 8:55). From that direct experience of God came a confident authority in his teaching in which he did not hesitate to announce a development in the hallowed precepts transmitted by tradition: "It was taught in the past, but now I say to you...." Such confidence in his relationships and teaching implies a breathtaking inner freedom.

One cannot read the Gospel of John without being deeply impressed with how Jesus' point of reference in everything is the will of his Father. One passage will suffice, though many others could be cited: "For this reason the Father loves me, because I lay down my life in order to take it up again. No one takes it from me, but I lay it down of my own accord. I have power to lay it down, and I have power to take it up again. I have received this command from my Father" (John 10:16, 17). These two verses, as does the whole of his life, clearly convey that personal autonomy and obedience to God are not incompatible.

In his inner self, Jesus was in constant and intimate dialogue with "Abba." From that deep place of security emerged an incredibly free and alive human being, finely attuned to the call of God in his life and ready to answer it with every fiber of his being. He knew who he was, where he came from, what his call was, and where he was going. Jesus retained his identity and his freedom while maintaining throughout his life an unswerving attachment to his Father's will.

You may have had the blessing of knowing someone whose life is "all in one place," organized around one center, who knows who she is, what she wants to do, and who is fully engaged in living it. Such a person is profoundly free and irresistibly alive. A person who is interiorly free calls others to freedom even without knowing it. Freedom attracts wherever it appears.

Stay Free from Unhealthy Attachments

A third constitutive element in spiritual freedom is freedom from inordinate attachments. "Inordinate attachments" is the term that frequently turns up in the classical writings of the great teachers of the spiritual life like Ignatius of Loyola, Teresa of Avila, and John of the Cross. It means that anyone who is serious about loving God totally must willingly entertain no self-centered pursuit of finite things sought for themselves, devoid of honest direction to God, our sole end. This teaching has firm roots in the New Testament. "So whether you eat or drink, or whatever you do, do everything for the glory of God," Paul wrote to the Corinthians (1:10:31). Whatever does mean whatever. The point at issue here is desiring or centering on something created *for its own sake alone.* We are to find delight in everything, but to cling to it in nothing. The saints had deep friendships, loved nature, art, food, and music, and found all of them to be mirrors of the divine which, of course, everything is meant to be.[10]

It is important to understand that "inordinate attachment" does not refer to experiencing pleasure in things; the avoidance of pleasure in human life is neither advisable nor possible. Nor does it refer simply to possessing or using things; we cannot avoid that either. Nor is being attracted, even powerfully so, to a beautiful person or object an unhealthy attachment. To be drawn to the splendors of creation is a compliment to the divine Artist. So what makes an attachment unhealthy? Here are three signs.[11]

The first sign is that the activity or thing is diverted from the purpose God intends for it. If, for example, I use my power of communication to tell a lie, I am subverting its social purpose to my own personal end of covering up a faulty action or to gain an advantage over another. My diversion of speech reveals that I am attached to something and trying to protect it. In short, I am clinging to it.

The second sign is excess in use. When we overeat, drink too much, recreate or work to the point of exhaustion, there is something disordered in our activity, and it cannot honestly be directed to the glory of God. These activities were not intended to make us sick. Or, to use another example, buying more clothes than needed may reveal an inordinate attachment to clothing or personal appearance.

The third sign of an unhealthy attachment is making means into ends. We have one ultimate purpose in life: to enter into full communion of life with the Trinity in our risen bodies. Everything else in the divine plan is oriented to bringing us into this final embrace with Beauty and Love. Eating, travel, entertainment, work, study, making love, art or music all have their place in turning our hearts and minds toward God. In God's scheme of things, they are all means. When we turn any one of them into an end in itself with no relation whatsoever to our Creator, we either have created an idol or are clinging to something created for our own self-centered sake. We may be so immersed in ourselves that we assume all sense pleasures are their own end, that we may pursue them aside from the very reason they exist: to plunge us into unending Beauty, Joy, Love, and Truth. The senses are given to us so that God might be more known and loved through them.

Daily Rededicate Your Life to God

The fourth theme in becoming spiritually free bids us to see, hear, and experience created realities in the service of God and not just for themselves. We let the gift always turn us in gratitude to the Giver. And we turn away from what shows no promise of leading us to God—reading material, activities, TV programs, movies that debase or stir up violent instincts within us rather than inspiring and ennobling us or making us laugh healthily at our creatureliness.

The goal here is freedom to move toward that which fulfills. Purifying ourselves of unhealthy attachments is a positive love matter: the pursuance of the Beloved in everything—eating, drinking, resting, working. Hopefully we will reach a point where we delight in working and resting, speaking and being silent, seeing and hearing, suffering and rejoicing, failing and succeeding, living and dying. All is to be directed to the Origin and Destiny of all.[12]

Spiritual Freedom in Action

Spiritual freedom, then, is like a diamond; it has different facets. It looks different depending on your angle of view, but every view contributes to a better overall appreciation of the diamond. In the Hebrew Scriptures the story of Job gives us a picture of what spiritual freedom looks like in the life of a person under extreme duress. If Job were a Texan, he would have owned half the Lone Star State and all the sheep, cattle, and oil wells thereon.

"This man," says the book of Job, "was the greatest of all the people of the east [read: southwest]." Besides that, he had a large family of beautiful children, seven sons and three daughters. He generously set them up, too: "His sons used to go and hold feasts in one another's houses...and invite their three sisters to eat and drink with them." Not only was Job rich in human and material terms, but he was a God-fearing man. Imagine the virtue required to have all the power such wealth represents and still be described as "blameless and upright" (Job 1:1–4). He was such a God-fearing man that after his sons and daughters held one of their parties, Job would get up early the following morning, find his way to a place of worship, and offer a sacrifice to God on their behalf just in case any of his children had lost their heads. God had good reason to be proud of Job.

But Satan wasn't convinced his virtue ran all that deep. "Give me leave to test him," he urges God. When permission is granted, Satan goes to work. In a first wave of disaster, Job sees his material possessions stolen or destroyed. In a second wave of tragedy, his beloved sons and daughters all perish in a natural disaster. And what is Job's response?

> Then Job arose, tore his robe, shaved his head, and fell on the ground and worshiped. He said, "Naked I came from my mother's womb, and naked shall I return there; the LORD gave, and the LORD has taken away; blessed be the name of the LORD." (Job 1:20, 21)

Job, it must be said, managed under great duress to keep first things first. He exemplifies what we have been describing. While in relationship to others, he knows who he is and is his own person; his first point of reference is his relationship to God as creature to Creator. Nor is he inordinately attached to his goods—he ascribed to his children and his material possessions their proper place as gift of God. He enjoys them while they are there and he lets them go when they are taken away.

The following story illustrates our fascination at and our desire for that kind of spiritual freedom:

> The great Buddhist saint Nagarjuna moved around naked except for a loincloth and, incongruously, a golden begging

bowl gifted to him by the King, who was his disciple. One night he was about to lie down to sleep among the ruins of an ancient monastery when he noticed a thief lurking behind one of the columns. "Here, take this," said Nagarjuna, holding out the begging bowl. "That way you won't disturb me once I have fallen asleep." The thief eagerly grabbed the bowl and made off—only to return the next morning with the bowl and a request. He said, "When you gave away this bowl so freely last night, you made me feel very poor. Teach me how to acquire the riches that make this kind of lighthearted detachment possible."[13]

We are edified by this story because we presume purity of intention on Nargajuna's part. It is precisely such motivation which reveals spiritual freedom. But we all know that a complex set of motivations can underlie the doing of a good deed. We may do it out of a need to appear good and generous in the eyes of others and thus have their approval, or out of a need to exercise power or control. These needs may provide the energy to do a good thing, but at the same time, they taint our fundamental motivation, rendering it more or less self-serving. It is precisely such personal needs that must be purified so that acts of generosity may truly be for the benefit of others rather than for personal gain. To the degree that we are able to govern and transcend these needs so that our behavior is not determined by them, we are free.[14]

Spiritual freedom could be described as the ability to think and act without external or internal compulsions. This is not meant to suggest that we can live without any pressures in our lives or that we can live as libertines without reference to the consequences of our action. Such license is, in reality, just another kind of slavery—to self-will. Freedom from internal compulsions means:

- Freedom from those habits of thought and action that hold us in chains;

- Freedom from our ego-centered activities and ambitions;

- Freedom from the various forms of self-meditation and escape into alcohol, sexual acting out, gambling, eating disorders, and workaholism;

- Freedom from being controlled by hatred, jealousy, envy, sloth, anger, and pride.[15]

This is the true freedom of heart for which we yearn. It is a gift of grace. It is the liberation offered by Jesus' death and resurrection and the gift of his Holy Spirit. But we have been set free *for* something, not just *from* something. We have been set free so that we in turn may help to liberate others from those things that bind them both externally (poverty, racism, illiteracy) and internally (behavioral patterns that lead to death). We have been set free so that we can continue the work of Jesus in the world, of giving concrete expression to God's reconciling, healing, life-giving presence and reign.[16] We have been set free for praise and thanksgiving, ultimately free to be ourselves: fallible, forgiven, confident in God's love, growing in the harvest of the Spirit which is "love, joy, peace, patience, kindness, generosity, faithfulness, gentleness, self-control" (Gal 5:22).

It is hard work to liberate oneself from inner compulsions and to commit oneself to the service of others or anything that transcends our own personal benefit and serves a wider world. But, as Jean Vanier, the founder of the l'Arche communities for the mentally disabled attests, this inner, spiritual freedom is not for an elite.

> For most people, like myself, it is something for which we have to work and struggle. It is a long but beautiful road. Some people seem to have fewer barriers, fewer defense mechanisms; their compulsions seem to be weaker. I have met wonderful mothers who seem whole and integrated. I have met wise and gentle men and women who are open and free. I have met people with disabilities who have an astounding freedom; they do not seem to be imprisoned in prejudice. I have met people with mental illness who are free in their hearts; they know they are ill, but they have understood and accepted their limits. I have met many people in slum areas and in broken situations all over the world who seem wonderfully free, uncluttered by the need for power and human glory....This freedom is for all. Some are closer to it. Others among us have to work harder for it, because we have stronger defenses to overcome.[17]

It is not the work of a month or a year, but it is the road that leads to life.

In the ensuing chapters, we will delve more deeply into the constitutive elements of spiritual freedom and explore each one's inner dynamics. We will also consider, through a variety of reflections, stories, and illustrations, what each one looks like when it is lived in concrete terms. And, at the end, several "tools for freedom" are offered as practical supports for the journey.

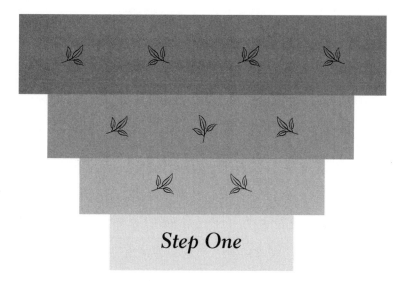

Know Who You Are

The Rendezvous

One's deepest self is like a timid fawn
that stays among the forest ferns
and only ventures forth at dawn.
One must patiently wait, with outstretched hand,
like a falconer standing straight and tall,
waiting for the feathered one to land.
One must create the sacred space
and order quests of lesser note
to be faithful to the time and place.
Then, constant to the rendezvous,
sit still and clear as morning dew
and your true self will be revealed to you.

2
Sightings of the True Self

In theological, philosophical, and psychological writings there are certain terms that one regularly encounters, like "person," "true self," "false self," "ego." Each one has a complex history and usage.[1] I first began encountering this language in the writings of Thomas Merton (1915–68), judged by many to be the most important spiritual writer of the twentieth century in the North American context. A Trappist monk, poet, peace and justice activist, Merton placed the true self at the center of his teaching on the Christian life.[2]

"For me, to be a saint means to be myself," Merton wrote in *Seeds of Contemplation.* Sanctity consists of "finding out who I am and of discovering my true self." What makes this difficult, is that "every one of us is shadowed by an illusory person: a false self...who wants to exist outside the radius of God's will and God's love—outside of reality and outside of life." The false self is an illusion "that exists only in my own egocentric desires." Unfortunately, for most of us the false self "is the fundamental reality of life to which everything else in the universe is ordered." Thus did Merton conclude to a paradoxical truth of life: "In order to become myself I must cease to be what I always thought I wanted to be, and in order to find myself, I must go out of myself, and in order to live I must die."[3]

The height of the paradox is love. Because God is love, a person "cannot enter into the deepest center of himself and thus pass through that center into God, unless he is able to pass entirely out of himself and empty himself to other people in the purity of a selfless love." Merton concluded that "love is my identity. Selflessness is my true self. Love is my true character. Love is my name." In the end, it all comes back to the true self: "If I find Him (God), I will find myself, and if I find my true self, I will find Him." But to find the true self we must first dispel the illusions created by the false self.[4]

Twelve years later, in his *New Seeds of Contemplation*, Merton characterizes the false self as the superficial consciousness of the external self, operating in opposition to the "deep transcendent self that awakens only in contemplation." He designates the superficial "I" of the external self as our empirical self, our individuality, our ego. This external, empirical self is not "the hidden and mysterious person in whom we subsist before the eyes of God." [5]

This is an explicitly theological interpretation, and Christian meanings of sin and grace are intrinsic to it. We are alienated from our inner self, the image of God in which we were created, by "the Fall" described symbolically in the Genesis account of creation. Our true, inner self must be saved from the false self by God's grace.

It is these notions of self, false self, and ego that I will work with in drawing out the importance of step one in the journey toward spiritual freedom: Know who you are. To denote the specialness of the true self as the "habitat of God," I will refer to it in the upper case simply as "Self."

Self

Every church or temple or synagogue has a sanctuary. It's the place where the meaning of the building comes clearest, where the essence of the sacred space is located. Particularly identified with the subject, the Holy One, for whom the building was erected, the sanctuary is the hallowed, inner space at the heart of the place. Self is somewhat like a sanctuary. It is here that God specially dwells.

Self is a conscious subject, the essence of our human interiority, "that" within us which is open to God and which recognizes God. There is no obstacle to union between God and Self; the union between the two exists at every moment in which God gives human existence. Hence, it is to be found in every "place" in which the human person exists, throughout one's corporeal being, and not just in the brain or the heart.

Self is an experience of a person's deepest reality as a subject, and as such, it is an experience of God insofar as God is immanent within Self. Yet, Self and God are not one. They are two different entities. At the same time, Self and God are united by means of God's gift of existence in each moment.

In his book *Zen Catholicism*, Dom Aelred Graham refers to the Self as God's habitat. This is not the same understanding of Self as is found in Hinduism, for example. The Upanishads, the final word on mystic experience uttered by the Vedas, stressed the ultimate reality, the eternal truth behind the ephemeral things of this world. The teachers of the Upanishads told their students to seek knowledge of the Atman, their true Self. The consummation of this knowledge was to know that the Self within was one with Brahman, the ultimate reality pervading all things. This was summed up in the statement "You are that"—that imperishable being, that immortal Reality, Brahman. The Atman or Self is the innermost divine soul in every creature.

The critical difference in Hindu and Christian understanding is that the Hindu would say, "I am divine," and the Christian would say, "I am united to the Divine, but I am not God." God is the one who gives the Self its existence, and Self is aware of having been given existence by God.

In diagram 1, there are three other words around the word Self: child of God, creature, sinner. Each one conveys something important about the Christian understanding of who we are. When the three are taken together and held in balance, we grasp more deeply the assertion in the outer triangle in the diagram: we are "one with God, but not God." We will briefly parse out the content of the essential characteristics attributed to us.

WHO AM I?

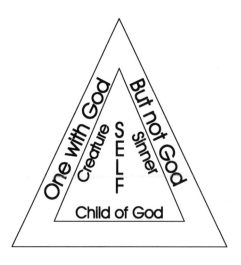

Creature

Our primary identity as creatures, as mortals, links us inextricably to God as our Creator. Jesuit psychologist Wilkie Au writes:

> "Creatures" and "creator" are co-relative terms. They cannot be properly understood apart from each other, just as "up" cannot be understood apart from "down." This is why Ignatius of Loyola taught that the foundation of our spiritual life must be a deep awareness of our basic identity: we are creatures whose very existence depends on the graciousness of a loving creator and Lord.[6]

Every creature of God is unique, interesting, fascinating. But by its nature, every mortal is also vulnerable, dependent, needy, finite, fallible. In short, every mortal has limitations. That is what distinguishes the creature from the Creator. The Navajo weavers never finish a work without allowing some defect, some imperfection in it. It is their way of remembering who they are as mortals.

In his small spiritual classic *Poverty of Spirit*, Johannes Metz writes about the "poverty of finiteness." The human spirit is transcendent, open to the universe, and has unlimited possibilities. In order to make something of ourselves through these possibilities, we have to make some decisions in order to gain a foothold in a historic, personal existence. But the very decision we make reveals our poverty, our finitude, for it involves the sacrifice and surrender of a thousand other possibilities. Our decision to answer a particular calling is effective only when we accept this risk of human poverty. The alternative is ceaseless experimentation.

And the poverty of our finiteness is also experienced in another way. The moment of decision is not always open to us or repeatable. There is a certain finality about it. There is a moment, an hour, when opportunity knocks and we can effect a necessary integration in order to move forward. But by the same token, because this opportunity is an "hour" and not an eternity, we can miss it.[7]

Adam and Eve demonstrate that reality. Talk of limitless possibilities! They had it all: communion with God, a love relationship with one another, and a harmonious existence with their total environment. That first part—communion with God—was key to all the rest. The serpent craftily tempted them with the words, "When you eat of the fruit of this tree, your eyes will be opened and you will be like God" (Gen 3:5). But they already were like God! They were made in God's image and likeness. The serpent was correct in implying that their eyes were closed, because they did not "see" it. And because they did not see it, they abused the gift of God's loving trust, and they lost it in its full integrity. They had been given everything they needed in that relationship. God's love was capable of fulfilling any of their desires. But they lost awareness of that love which wanted to share everything with them.

This story is a wonderful example of myth—a story that is not necessarily true on the outside, but it is true on the inside. "Inside" this story is the truth that our sinful disorders are connected to a lack of awareness of God's love. As so many of the mystics have declared, we already have everything but we don't know it and we don't experience it. Everything has been given to us. We have to start where we are and deepen what we already have by coming to awareness of it. Then we realize that we are already there.

Sinner

Biblical Judaism had several concrete expressions for sin and saw it as a rupture of a relationship. The Jews symbolized sin by active metaphors: missing the mark, straying, rebellion, deviation, turning away, going off to a far country. In his own study of the symbolism of evil, Paul Ricoeur confirms that sin is a religious reality before being an ethical one. It is not first the transgression of an abstract rule, but the violation of a personal bond.[8]

Sin is primarily a symbol that explores one fact of our life before God. Just as "grace" symbolizes our union with God, "sin" symbolizes our alienation from God. It is the word used in the Judaeo-Christian tradition to describe the abuse of the freedom given by God to creative and responsible persons. We are endowed by God with the inestimable gift of freedom, and we sometimes misuse our power. Howard Gray paints a graphic picture of how sinful behavior leads to a damned existence:

> When you cut it all away, gossiping about people so that we ruin their chances for advancement, for living in a neighborhood, or for making friends is a pretty damned thing to do. Being cruel to my children so that I only love them if they do the things I want, and I only praise them when they flatter me, is a pretty damned way to raise kids, and it's a good way to make them screwed up for the rest of their lives. Building an economy on the bodies of women and little

children in a pornographic or prostitution ring is a pretty damned way to make a living....Take away the sophistication, perfume, soft lights, and the glossy print—take away all of the conventionalities that allow us to live with bribery and lying and manipulation...and you see something that is not very pleasant and of which we should be ashamed...[something] very discordant in the kind of harmony God intended.[9]

We can all recognize the world in which we live in those examples of specific sinful acts. What we are concerned with here, however, are not sinful acts as such, but getting a sense of what the *condition* of "being a sinner" looks and feels like. An important distinction needs to be made between the two.

Sinfulness and Sin: Two Different Diagnostics

Suppose we have grown in the awareness of God's presence and love and do not commit a lot of flagrant sinful acts. When we apply a fine-grained attentiveness, however, to the subtle and spontaneous movements of the heart, a distressing inclination to self-centeredness is perceived. When I sit at table with a heavy person who has a plate stacked with food, I may become aware of a spontaneous, judgmental, and self-righteous movement within myself as the words pop up in mind, "No wonder she's so fat...." I know I didn't *will* that thought, but it came from *somewhere* inside of me.

When, in the context of family or community life, I put some food that I have enjoyed but not finished back in the refrigerator—

way back in the refrigerator, hoping that no one else will see it and that I will be able to enjoy it again at some later point, what is manifesting in that spontaneous action is a heart movement of selfishness, a movement toward hoarding rather than sharing.

When I see a need posted in the bulletin or on the bulletin board that I have the time and ability to respond to but leave it to somebody else to do, my own convenience continues to be the sun around which everything else revolves in my personal solar system.

When I am engaged in taking care of something that needs attention and subconsciously do it in such a way or at such a time that others will see me doing it and express their appreciation, my desire for approval or for the esteem of others guides my activity.

These thoughts and acts themselves are so subtle and so quick that oftentimes they pass unnoticed. They are not sinful acts as such. They are rather movements of the heart that come from a place deep within us and that reveal something to us about ourselves. When we tune in to them and watch them, even for the span of a few days, they seem to be so regular that we despair of ever effectively uprooting all of them. We finally accept that there is something about our *condition*, there is something in our *state of being*, that is always thinking "me first!," always setting things up so that we will get what we want or that others will see that our way is best. This is what the apostle Paul was describing when he wrote,

> I do not understand my own actions. For I do not do what I want but I do the very thing I hate....So I find it to be a law that when I want to do what is good, evil lies close at

hand. For I delight in the law of God in my inmost self, but I see in my members another law at war with the law of my mind, making me captive to the law of sin that dwells in my members. (Rom 7:15, 21–23)

One of the most dramatic cameos in the gospels of what the interplay of these two "laws" looks like in action is the exchange between Jesus and his apostles near the end of the last supper, and events a few hours later:

Peter said to him, "Though all become deserters because of you, I will never desert you." Jesus said to him, "Truly I tell you, this very night, before the cock crows, you will deny me three times." Peter said to him, "Even though I must die with you, I will not deny you." And so said all the disciples. (Matt 28:33–35)

There's the clear statement of intention, what they *want* to do. Thirty verses and a scant few hours later when the crowd arrives with swords and clubs in the garden of Gethsemane to apprehend Jesus, the same gospel baldly states: "Then all the disciples deserted him and fled" (28:56). That's the human condition. When push comes to shove, more often than not we will look out for number one and act to save our skin.

When we discover that "war" within ourselves between our good intention and what we in fact end up doing, we have come face to face with what the theological tradition describes as "being a sinner." It simply means to say that the organism is not functioning correctly according to the original design. Somewhere in the hookup, a wire is loose. This condition does not nullify our being beloved children of God. But it does mean that constant vigilance of our thoughts and feelings will be required in order that we might act in godly ways according to our best intentions.

Sinful Acts: A Different Analysis

Sins, or sinful acts, require a different analysis. The first association most of us have with sin is guilt. We know guilt feels bad, so sin, its cause, is not something we want to even think about. The knee-jerk reaction is that sin is a negative concept that has done a lot of harm to people by burdening them with guilt: "So don't talk to me about it. Don't even mention it!" The solution to this problem is not to throw out the whole notion of sin, but to understand more clearly what it does to us. Only then can we relate to it with an appreciation for its role in the overall scheme of things.

The place where we start and the place where we end is always love. The true import of sin is that it renders us helpless to receive and to return love. Some examples: If I start a fight in which others are injured, whether physically or emotionally, I have put myself in a position where it will be extremely difficult for others to offer me the love I need and want. If I steal another person's material goods or come between spouses, I will be resented if not hated, when it is really love I want. If I lie, it makes it doubly difficult for others to trust me.

When my behavior is such, I am my own worst enemy where the realization of my life project is concerned. I want to be close to others, but my actions result in distancing me from them. I am embarked on the long journey of life, want good companions and need to keep myself in good walking condition, and at the same time I alienate others from me and shoot myself in the foot. With my own actions, I paint myself into a corner and, once there, I can't get out and others can't get in. I am helpless. This is what sin does to us.

God *is* love and wants nothing more than to give us love. But when we engage in behavior that traps us, we're not well positioned to even *receive* love, much less give it. That is what must wound the heart of God most of all: that we use our freedom to cut ourselves off from what we most need and God most wants to give. When we have fallen down that well, we need help. We need someone who will throw us a rope.

There are attitudes and dispositions, habits of mind and behavior, patterns of thought and feeling, dependencies and attachments, weights and burdens from the past that trap and imprison us. That is why we need a savior God.

Martin Luther understood this from the dregs of his own personal struggle and experience, and he came up out of the well roaring. "We are not saved by our own efforts, but by faith in the grace of God!" It became the battle cry of the Protestant Reformation. It has taken Lutherans and Catholics 450 years to formally agree to that in a document signed by the authorities of the Vatican and the Lutheran World Federation in Augsburg, Germany, on October 31, 1999. A lot of Catholics still need to accept it in their hearts. But it is only through the experience of helplessness and powerlessness that we experience the meaning of grace. If we have never touched that experience or admitted it into awareness, we haven't yet looked deeply and honestly enough within. Denying the experience of our own impotency is not the solution. "The gravest sin," said Paul Claudel, "is to lose the sense of sin."

But sin is never the last word. "Where sin increased, grace abounded all the more" (Rom 5:20). The last and loudest word is always God's love for us. The parable of the prodigal son shows what Jesus understands by sin. It is going out from the father's house to seek happiness in the world with all its shallow desires. By the same story, he shows that penitence is the way to God as the Father who receives the sinner with love. Jesus described his task to the Pharisees in the words, "I have come to call not the righteous but sinners" (Matt 9:13). He knows that he is sent to those who live in guilt and estrangement from God in order to call them to God. His attitude is expressed in the closest fellowship known to the oriental world—table fellowship. He is establishing a new fellowship with God by drawing sinners into fellowship with himself.[10]

One of the things that distinguishes Christianity from the standpoint of religious history and theology is its attitude to sin. Buddhism speaks of the abuse of human freedom in terms of ignorance.[11] As for the notion of sin in Hinduism, early scriptures have a strong but very nonpersonal concept of a violation of the divine order, in which an individual steps outside the bounds of established social norms or fails to perform proper ritual. The sense of genuine moral, rather than physical or cosmic, evil begins to emerge in the Upanishads, but it is still seen rather as a failure in knowledge than a transgression against a divine reality. In the Bhagavad Gita, too, sin amounts to a failure of intention whereby one acts out of selfish or ulterior motives rather than a sense of duty.[12]

Scripture scholars R. Reitzenstein and G. Kittel reflect Christianity's distinctive understanding when they say:

> Christianity is the religion of the sinner. The sinner stands before God, and God wants the sinner….It is the religion at whose heart stands the consciousness of not having done what one ought to have done, i.e., the consciousness of sin….The message of forgiveness is always for early Christianity the message of Christ.[13]

The apostle Paul was the theologian who raised the question of sin as a power that impacts our nature and that of the world. Paul saw the Christ event coming upon men and women in their specific reality as sinners. It comes upon them as an event that rescues them from this reality and reconstitutes them. The Christ event means for humanity the overcoming of sin and the beginning of the dominion of life. This is the cosmic alteration effected by Christ. Meanwhile, however, the Christian stands in the tension of a double reality: basically redeemed from sin, reconciled and freed, but still actually at war with sin, threatened, attacked and placed in jeopardy by it.[14]

Christianity breathes with two lungs, the Western and the Eastern, which means that there is within Christianity a legitimate plurality of faith understanding and expression. Christian thinking on sin and the extent to which our nature is affected by it is a case in point. The Christian East adopts a different theological anthropology from most of Western Christianity, both Catholic and Protestant. The Western Church tended to be more pessimistic about humankind's plight than was the Eastern Church. The Christian West taught a doctrine of original sin that included the notion of humankind's physical solidarity with Adam and its participation in Adam's sinful act. This was largely absent in Eastern thinking.[15]

Eastern Orthodox, Roman Catholic, and most Protestant Christians share a common general answer to the question of "What's wrong with humanity?" All share a biblical and experiential recognition that humanity lives outside of communion with God, that this lack of communion prevents us from being *truly* human, and that this state of separation from God is called, in shorthand, "sin." There are important differences, however, in the three traditions' understanding of how we have come to exist in this state, and how seriously it has affected our human nature. In short, there are different theologies of "original sin." Eastern Christians, for example, reject any notion of inherited "original guilt"—the notion that all humans share the guilt of Adam's sin. The Christian East consistently recognizes the effects of "ancestral sin" in terms of human mortality and a difficulty in maintaining an unwavering communion with God, but it has never accepted Augustine's argument that all humanity inherits the guilt of Adam. [16]

The Greek Fathers developed a more generous anthropology, even for fallen human nature, around the biblical teaching that we are made in the image of God. The divine imprint may be obscured, but it is still intact. Our natural free will is oriented toward God precisely because humanity is created *by* God in *God's own image.* The brilliant seventh-century Greek theologian Maximos the Confessor emphasized how orientation toward God is at the heart of our human nature. The problem of our fallen condition is that, because we have broken communion with God, our spiritual vision has become "clouded" so that we fail to recognize clearly in what direction our natural orientation lies and therefore fail to move consistently in the direction of restored communion with God.[17]

Greek Orthodox theologian Dr. Valerie Karras puts it this way:

> Orthodoxy understands human sin primarily not as deliberate and willful opposition to God, but rather as an inability to know ourselves and God clearly. It is as though God were calling out to us and coming after us in a storm, but we thought we heard his voice in another direction and kept moving away from him, either directly or obliquely. It is illuminating that the Greek word for sin, *hamartia*, means to "miss the mark." Despite our orientation toward God, we "miss the mark" because, not only does the clouded spiritual vision of our fallen condition make it difficult for us to see God clearly, but we fail to understand even ourselves truly; thus, we constantly do things which make us feel only incompletely and unsatisfactorily good or happy because we don't recognize that God is himself the fulfillment of our innate desire and natural movement.[18]

In Eastern Christian understanding, the eternal Son of God took on our fallen nature, including our mortality, in order to restore it to the possibility of immortality. For Orthodox Christians, God is not a judge in a courtroom and Christ did not die in order to pay the legal penalty or "fine" for our sins. Jesus died *so that* he might be resurrected. Just as he is one nature with the Father in his divinity, we are one nature with him in his humanity. Through our sharing of his crucified *and* resurrected human nature, our own human nature is transformed from mortality to immortality. God's initiative and action in the creation of humanity in the image of God, and in the incarnation, cross, and resurrection, are of universal significance to humanity and cosmic significance to the creation as a whole. The potential for immortality and communion with God, lost in the Fall, is restored to *all* because all human beings share the human nature of Jesus Christ which was restored in the resurrection.[19]

For both Eastern and Western Christians, the foundational truth of the biblical tradition is that, despite every failing in our lives, the roots of our being remain in the goodness of God. The essence of who we are has not been erased by sin but obscured by it. One analogy would be that of a beautiful plant, suffering from blight. Botanists in examining it would define it in terms of its essential features and its life-force, not in terms of its blight. The blight would be described as foreign to the plant, as attacking its essence. The same analysis holds when it comes to defining what is deepest within us. In our Western Christian tradition we have tended to understand human nature in terms of its blight. Rather than seeing ourselves as essentially sinful, the Eastern Christian perspective sees sin as but a blight attacking the essence of our being.[20] Our essence partakes of a beauty that is deeper than any ugliness in our lives. What is deepest in us is our beauty as sons and daughters of God.

Child of God

We are created for relationship and into relationship. We are created for relationship because the Trinity wanted to share intimate love with us. We are created into relationship because God is personally involved in each of our lives, nurturing and guiding us. The deepest desire of our hearts is for God. And the deepest desire of God's heart is for us. God calls us son, daughter, precious, beautiful. God reverences us, exalts over us. And we respond with the equally intimate and relational language used by Jesus: "Abba, Father."

The core moment of Jesus' public life was the baptism in the Jordan, when he heard the affirmation, "You are my Son, the Beloved; with you I am well pleased" (Matt 1:11). That is Jesus' core experience. He is reminded in a deep way of who he is. The temptations in the desert are attempts to move him away from that spiritual identity, to get him to think that he is someone else—one who can turn stone into bread, jump from the temple, make others bow to his power. But he stays close to his essential identity: the beloved of God. Throughout the events of his public ministry in which he is both honored and rejected, he stays grounded in that identity: "You are my Son, the Beloved."

My mother has a spontaneous gesture that conveys for me this loving attitude of God toward us. When months have gone by since my last visit home and I arrive, she sometimes takes my face in her two hands and says, "Let me look at you." It is a wonderful thing to be held in the gaze of loving eyes. That's what I imagine God does with each of us: tenderly holds our face and says, "Let me look at you." It's a privilege to be a son of my parents, but it's an even greater privilege to be a child of God.

A friend, Sister Karen Doyle, shared this story from her own life. Born to two of her friends were twins, joined at the head. They shared part of the same brain. On her way over to her friends' home she was nervous because she didn't know how she would react when she actually saw the children. The mother met her at the door, full of excitement, and took her into the room where the children lay. "Pick them up, Karen," she said, "and bring them here to me on my lap." As soon as she experienced the children through their mother's loving eyes, her nervousness fell away. "Look," the mother said, cradling their toes, "how perfectly formed they are!" And she kissed their little feet. Then she took their hands, and exclaimed, "Look at these tiny fingers—how perfectly they are formed." And she kissed their hands. Then she ran a finger around their ears, similarly exclaiming how perfect and marvelously formed they were, and kissed them. When she came to their heads, she said, "And this—we can work with this, Karen, we can work with this." And she kissed their heads. That is how we are related to as God's children. God looks upon us with immense love and relishes all that is well formed in us. When God comes to the place where we are most vulnerable, God kisses it tenderly and says, "And this—we can work with this. We can work with this."

All the love and acceptance we need is freely, generously offered. Our recognition of God's unconditional love toward us as a constant, efficacious presence helps to set us free from shame, guilt, anxiety, and fear to be the people God intended us to be. When sins are forgiven, they are not so much erased as accepted and transformed. It is the same for the sinner. Our sinfulness is not eliminated (there is always concupiscence, the inclination to evil), but accepted and transformed. Unlike the contemporary tendency to absolutize fulfillment as the be-all and end-all of human existence, Christian faith postulates that the treasure chest at the end of the trail is full of the riches of forgiveness. When forgiveness, and not fulfillment, is seen as the final page in the story of our lives, we can live with our weaknesses in confidence and trust that God's grace will bring to completion the good work begun in us. The poignant story of the prodigal son provides the image by which to live: we will enjoy the unconditional acceptance of God not because we are perfect, but *in spite of* our imperfections. We do not need to live up to any conditions of worth, nor will the inadequacy of our efforts condemn us. The promise of ultimate forgiveness allows us to be at one and the same time incomplete and complete, flawed and yet accepted. [21]

When Jesus appears to the women who went to the tomb as the first day of the week was dawning, "they came to him, took hold of his feet and worshiped him. Then Jesus said to them, 'Do not be afraid; go and tell my brothers to go to Galilee; there they will see me'" (Matt 28:9–10). Note well he does not say: "Go, tell those who fell asleep in the garden when I most needed their support." Nor: "Go, tell those who deserted me and fled when they came to take me." But: "Go, tell my *brothers*...." There is only forgiveness, understanding, and acceptance in that term of endearment.

You may know of a family situation in which a parent, greatly displeased by the actions of a child, refused to speak to and perhaps even see the son or daughter, declaring in extreme cases, "I have no son! (or daughter)." It is not unheard of for someone to be set adrift from their family, effectively cut off from communication, affection, support. At the time of Jesus, children could be disinherited in this way—except in one case. If you had been adopted, you could never be cut off. Having been chosen, you had a permanent position in the family. You could walk away from the family, but you could never be disowned.[22] That is what it means for us to be children of God, for by God's generous love we have been adopted, chosen, and are irrevocably members of

God's family. Paul says as much in reflecting on all his Jewish brothers and sisters who have not accepted Jesus as God's anointed one: "I ask, then, has God rejected his people? By no means! …as regards election, they are beloved…for the gifts and the calling of God are irrevocable" (Rom 11:1, 28, 29).

Such acceptance liberates us to live free from the compulsive need to perfectly actualize our human potential, and it releases us from the guilt that results from coming up short of our ambitious aspirations. Success and failure are dossiers that will never be inspected. The folder God is interested in is the one marked "Trust in God."

Knowing who I am is like a battery. It has a positive pole and a negative pole. The negative pole is like a stop sign at a railroad crossing. It tells us to stop, look, and listen. Do I read it? Or do I ignore it and just keep going? Awareness of myself as creature and sinner is one pole of self-knowledge. Awareness of myself as child of God is the other. Unless both ends of the battery are hooked up, there is no current. Unless I have a visceral experience of my creature/sinner pole and accept it as part (not all, just part) of my reality, I will resist in one way or another accepting that, while I am one with God, I am not God. Such grounding in reality is what true humility is all about.

In our identity as Christians, we hold all three together. In the Catholic eucharistic rite, there is a prayer that exemplifies this. Just before advancing to receive communion, the congregation paraphrases the words of the Roman centurion who asked Jesus to heal his sick servant: "Lord, I am not worthy to have you come under my roof" (Matt 8:8). In our capacity as creatures and sinners, that's true. But then we proceed to receive in our capacity as children of God. That's true, too. We are loved with an ever-lasting love.

The gospel of Christ is given to tell us what we have forgotten, and that is who we are. In the spiritual life it is not a question of being told what to do, but of being reminded of who we are. Only when we know who we are will we see more clearly what we should do. The grace of repentance is not about turning around in order to become someone other than ourselves; rather, it is about turning around in order to be restored to what is deepest and best in us. The problem is not human nature, but our living at a distance from true human nature. Grace restores us again to ourselves.[23] As John Meyendorff observed, "'natural' human life presupposes communion with God."[24]

This Eastern Christian understanding of communion with God connotes a true union which, like the appearance of Christ on Mount Tabor, transfigures and deifies our human nature. In a succinct and explicit articulation of this doctrine, known as *theosis* (deification), the early church father Athanasius declared that Christ became human in order that we might be deified. *Theosis* is not just the "goal" of salvation; it *is* salvation in its essence and fulfillment. Restoration to the potentiality of Adam and Eve is just a starting point. We are called to communion with God, to grow and mature into the likeness of God, to become "deified" by participation in God's own life through the Holy Spirit.[25]

To say that we are called to grow and mature into the likeness of God, that we are made in the image of God, that we are children of God is to say that the knowledge of our true selves is linked inseparably with the knowledge of God. The fourteenth-century English mystic Julian of Norwich recorded in one of her

"Revelations of Divine Love" that "I saw no difference between God and our essence, but it was all God." At the heart of her soul she sees Christ, entirely at home. "Our soul is so deeply founded in God," she says, "that we cannot acquire knowledge of it until we have knowledge of God, its creator, to whom it belongs."[26] Only in seeking the dwelling place of God will we find our true selves.

The ninth-century Irish teacher John Scotus Eriugena called Christ "our epiphany." Not only is he the epiphany, the manifestation, of God, but he is *our* epiphany, manifesting what is deepest in us—the image of God. He reflects the mystery of God's being to us as well as the mystery of our own being. To be made in the image of God is essentially to be mystery. In Christ we both see the face of God and our own true face.[27] The truth of who we are is "hid with Christ in God," as St. Paul says (Col 3:3). The gospel is given to us to lead us into the true depths of the mystery of God's image within us. Grace is given to us to reunite us to something at the very core of our being and to restore us to the beauty of our God-given nature. Grace is given to make us truly ourselves.

3
Ego and the False Self

In popular usage, "ego" does not generally carry a positive connotation. We might make comments as to how egotistical he is or how her ego needs to be taken down a couple of notches. Ego is seldom ascribed to someone in a complimentary fashion. That is unfortunate, because without what we shall call here the ego, we could not exist in the real world (see diagram 2).

WHO AM I?

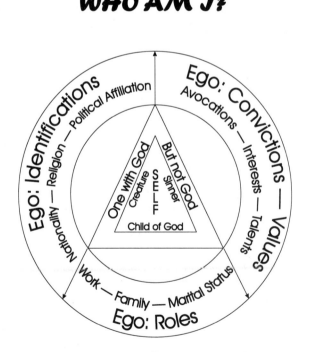

In his book *The Desiring Self*, Walter Conn develops the premise that our fundamental desire is to transcend ourselves in relationship: to the world, to others, and to God. But only those who have a developed, powerful sense of themselves have the strength to realize significant transcendence. In this fundamental human desire, there are two focal points: first, the drive to develop a sense of ourselves, a center of strength; and second, the dynamism to move beyond ourselves in relationship.[1] In my usage here, ego describes that "sense of ourselves," that "center of strength" through which we interface with the world.

Ego is the individual, intentional, active, and responsible agent of Self. Without the ego, the Self's potential cannot be developed and expressed. Ego's relationship to Self is like that of a tree branch to its trunk. They are not really two different entities, but neither do Self and ego have the same experience of human subjectivity. The trunk represents the vast potentiality of human consciousness, which is always present to the ego, but which is for the most part "underground," that is, subconscious. The ego is rooted in Self and emanates from it, but for the most part it is turned toward the world "above ground" (conscious).

Through the process of engagement with the outside world, ego forges its identity and its story. Whereas the language of Self is dreams, spontaneous fantasies, and intuitive hunches, the language of ego is generally that of the surrounding culture in the outside world that is its environment. Each new experience reveals more to it about "who I am" as regards, for example, its gifts, wounds, and motives. Ego is one's personal, individual consciousness. Ego's form or structure is reflected in self-image.

Ego's self-image is derived from the picture it has of itself as a result of its life experiences. In diagram 2, my various identifications (American/Canadian, Roman Catholic, Paulist, Irish-German), particular roles (son, brother, friend, priest, ecumenist), and the sundry judgments or convictions that I hold about myself (athletic, contemplative, lover-of-life, poetic) all run together to make up my image of myself. Ego tends to make its choices by referring to self-image. For example, if you see yourself as reclusive and shy and you are invited to become part of a new act on the big stage at Caesar's Palace, you will likely decline. The image we have of ourselves shapes our choices.

The key feature to note about ego and its self-image is that all the identifications, convictions, and roles that comprise it are subject to change. All of them are dependent on events outside themselves. If I live in Quebec and identify myself as a Canadian, and Quebec separates from Canada, what then? If I hang my identity upon my role as ecumenical officer for my community and then it asks me to go into parish work, who am I then? If I identify myself as athletic and am crippled in a car accident that renders me quadriplegic for the rest of my life, what is my identity then?

Most people would recognize that even when external conditions change, there is always a part of ourselves, an inner core, that perdures and continues to shape our external persona. If an athletic person is crippled, her spirit of discipline and hard work will nonetheless influence her chances for recovery. In other words, ego shapes the way one's Self will be expressed.

It is important for us to recognize ego's role in the overall scheme of things because our tendency is to allow the content of ego's self-image to fill up our sense of who we are, when upon reflection we quickly see that there is much more. There is no ego experience when we sleep, for example, and yet we know that we still exist. So even when ego is "turned off," there is a deeper strata to who we are that continues to sustain our existence.[2]

This understanding of ego is what Merton had in mind when he wrote:

> We must remember that this superficial "I" is not our real self. It is our "individuality" and our "empirical self" but it is not truly the hidden and mysterious person in whom we subsist before the eyes of God. The "I" that works in the world, thinks about itself, observes its own reactions and talks about itself is not the true "I" that has been united to God in Christ. It is at best the vesture, the mask, the disguise of that mysterious and unknown "self" whom most of us never discover until we are dead. Our external, superficial self is not eternal, not spiritual. Far from it. This self is doomed to disappear as completely as smoke from a chimney. It is utterly frail and evanescent.[3]

False Self

The false self is a system of mental and emotional programming that we develop to cope with the lack of love and acceptance, with the fear, shame, distrust, and resentment that ensue from being loved conditionally. The problem is not the existence of ego, but its formation in the context of conditional love. The false self is a survival system designed to cope with the emotional trauma of early childhood. It seeks happiness in satisfying the instinctual needs of survival/security, affection/esteem, and power/control.[4] Stephen Cope describes it in these terms:

When, at any stage of development, a child's energy, needs, and particular self cannot be adequately received by her parents, her siblings and her social environment, she may make an unconscious "script decision." She says, in effect, "The way I am is not alright. I must be another way." She becomes disconnected from her ability to savor the experience of the self just the way it is. She cannot sustain a sense of the rightness of the world. She feels, rather, the wrongness of herself. Her energy begins to focus on "how I should be" as a concept or an image, and then on manifesting that image of the self. After that, her life becomes an attempt to undo her chronic sense of wrongness....The false self is born when the environment does not welcome the self to be as it is.[5]

We all operate out of our false self to some extent. It's a set of ideas we carry around inside ourselves that tells us how to dress and talk, what TV programs to watch, where to go on holiday — if, of course, we want to be accepted. We absorb these messages from people whose esteem we want, from advertisements that assure us of popularity if we eat this or drink that. These messages insinuate themselves into our life script with only marginal awareness on our part. Before we know it, we're dancing to their tune.

The false self is the syndrome of our emotional programs for happiness grown into sources of motivation. Our need to be accepted and our need for affection, for example, are valid needs, but it is important to know when we are ensnared by them and when we are free. When the need becomes exaggerated or when we follow these subconscious scripts without consciously reviewing and affirming them, we can lose our freedom or we can find ourselves manipulating other people in order to get what we want. Or we may steel ourselves against the world out of a sense of sheer survival. It's only when these needs and how they drive us are exposed to the light of day and brought into conscious awareness that we are ready to discover and embrace who we are at a deeper level. In the words of a friend, Philomene Kocher, it is "the way of acceptance." Here is how she tells her story:

> Voice. My voice. How I struggled as a young adult to even recognize its existence. Working hard. Keeping busy. There was no time to slow down, to stop and listen to the inner voice.
>
> Until my mother died and my world blew apart. During the first months of inner darkness, there was no choice but to slow down as fatigue became a constant companion. I stared out the window hoping to find solace. I watched the sun change its place on the limestone wall as summer turned to fall turned to winter. As I slowly climbed out of the pit, I vowed that I would put the pieces of my life back together differently.
>
> I eventually found my way to a gifted counselor. From our first meeting when I began to share my story, I knew that she would provide a safe place for healing. My brittle pain began to quiver that day, but it would be a long time before it would break and begin to ease.
>
> Oh, how I tested her. The quiet strength through her words and through the spaces she held for my words became a lightening rod for me as I rolled into and out of

storms that shook my foundation. And my words were heard. Again and again and again. Without judgment. Even when I would have the courage to share the "worst" parts of myself, there was no judgment. It was a long time before I could begin to see that the "worst" was actually the "most wounded." And my pain began to ease when I realized that I didn't need fixing, but that I needed to accept myself with compassion.

Perhaps most of all, though, it was through the dream groups the counselor facilitated that brought me home to the gift of being heard. We each had a chance to check in, and in a few minutes share what had been happening during the week. We each then shared a dream. There were no comments given during these rounds; we simply shared in turn. There was something special about speaking and being heard without judgment. It was several weeks before I could relax and joke with the group, "Did I check in okay? I'm so nervous." Week after week, we spoke into the silence. It was a powerful experience to know that this sacred space was available for me to learn how to share from my heart. To share and to be received. To be silent and to receive. To recognize what was unspoken in the words from my mouth, and to hear what was unspoken in the voices of others. The eight weeks of the dream circle taught me lessons that resonated to my bones. I began to just be, learning to accept my own voice and myself with less judgment and more compassion.

My life *is* different now. I encountered a wise woman in my counselor, and she helped me to patiently seek the Wise One in myself. She listened with intention, and I could "hear" myself being listened to. And that knowing of a new way, the way of acceptance, trickled down and touched the bedrock of my being.

"I needed to accept myself with compassion." Compassion is maturity, and maturity is acceptance—the acceptance of oneself with one's own flaws, as well as of others with theirs. To be free is to know who we are, with all that is both beautiful and broken within us. It is to love our own values, to embrace them and cultivate them. When we are anchored in an understanding of who we are and are at the same time open to others, we are free to change.[6]

No Clean Slate

From infancy on, we are shaped by our environment at an emotional level. It is undoubtedly rooted in the fact that without food, without love, we die. We begin completely dependent on our environment. One of the ways the false self finds expression is in making us believe that we are totally dependent on others even after we have sufficient maturity to feed ourselves, to love and be loved, and to organize our lives. It deludes us into thinking that we are *only* creatures of our environment, with no relationship to a Totally Other. Is not that what "being like little children" meant for Jesus—to recognize that we are dependant upon Another for everything?

The false self is artful in attaining its agenda: feeling good, feeling secure, feeling in control. We were born addicted to our feelings. If it felt good, we wanted it; if it felt bad, we didn't want it. Our memory banks have on file everything that occurred from the womb to the present, especially memories with strong emotional charges. The biocomputers of our brains and nervous systems have been developing emotional programs for happiness from the first years of our life—happiness at this stage meaning the prompt fulfillment of our instinctual needs. By the time we come to the age of reason and develop reflective self-consciousness around the age of twelve or thirteen, we have in place fully developed emotional programs for happiness based on the emotional judgments of the infant and the child. About the time we are cultivating an active interest in the spiritual life, we come to realize that we do not start the spiritual journey with a clean slate. We carry with us a prepackaged set of values and preconceived ideas that, unless confronted and redirected, will soon take our journey off the rails. As psychotherapist Stephen Cope writes,

> Among the many brilliant insights brought into our culture in this century by psychoanalysis, this is perhaps the simplest, and the most important: Much of mental and emotional life is unconscious. It happens completely outside of our conscious awareness. Most reasonably educated Americans now give lip service to this insight. We know about slips of the tongue, dreams, accidents, and "forgetting." We know, at least theoretically, how the unconscious leaks out. We know about what Freud called "the return of the repressed." But when we actually do meet the unconscious at work in our daily dramas…, it can be astonishing. Most of us, most of the time, cannot bear to acknowledge that we live up to our necks in the dark waters of unconsciousness. We spend our

days acting out little dramas driven from the dark recesses of the self.[7]

The new, middle ring in diagram 3 represents our life experience, some of which we are aware of and "own" (conscious), some of which has been repressed but we know is down there in the shadows (the unconscious), and some of which was suppressed because it was too traumatic and we have blotted it out of our consciousness altogether. In this middle ring between Self and ego is our life experience. It is the door through which the false self enters upon the stage of our existence.

WHO AM I?

The Ideal vs. the Real World

In an ideal world, all our life experience would be positive. The Self would guide and direct the developmental formation of ego by continually mediating a sense of God's presence through our continuous life experience of unconditional love. In growing up, however, none of us breathed the pure air of unconditional love. When we instead picked up a feeling of being loved conditionally, for what we did, rather than simply for who we were, we concluded that we were only lovable and acceptable if we did the right things.

We then became alert to the signals in our environment that cued us in as to what kinds of things brought us the security of love and acceptance. It is at this point that our ego turned outward and started relying more on the signals from the environment than from the messages emanating from the Self. The outer environment may have been saying "good marks," "slim," "lots of money," "dress well," "say the right things," "go to the 'in' places"—"these are the things that will bring you happiness!" The messages coming from Self did not have the same persuasive power to deliver the goods of prompt fulfillment of our instinctual needs: survival/security; affection/esteem; power/control.

The result: Ego grows distant from Self and begins to march more and more according to the signals coming in from the false self, which is working full time to see that those deep-seated security needs are met always and everywhere. Plainly put, the false self is a hijacked ego, a plane on an errant flight path with a bogus pilot who has broken off communication with the control tower (Self). As communication between ego and Self atrophies, ego loses touch with the presence of God in the ground of its being and forgets who it really is. To compensate, it identifies strongly with family, country, civic group, political party, sports team, circle of friends and takes its cues from there.

This whole system, built up to protect us against the fear that ensues from the experience of being loved conditionally, is the false self system.[8] It is this system, not the ego, that goes by the name of false self. It is not false in the sense of unreal; what is false about it is that it has turned ego's perception of what makes for genuine happiness toward things that will ultimately disappear or disappoint.

The advertising industry invests millions in catering to the false self. Trish, who has participated in a few of my retreats, works for a big ad agency. She explains how it works:

My job is to leverage human motivations and to build advertising that will "catch" consumers and get them to buy certain products and services. We do this by understanding motivations and needs on a macro level and then attempting to create an emotional connection with consumers based on these needs. The emotional connection is usually created by developing an image which surrounds the product yet is largely unrelated to that product.

The image is often one that leverages people's needs for acceptance, love, approval; in other words to fill the God-shaped hole which exists in our hearts. To do this we show perfect, popular, rich people and associate that with a product to say that if you use this brand of product you will by association be popular, loved, sexy, rich (the process of classical conditioning).

The false self is a reliable customer; a whole industry caters to it. For those who try to bring their spirituality into the workplace, however, it is a field of tension. Trish witnesses to the inner-world/outer-world struggle that is familiar to many in the marketplace:

> I feel conflicted at times working in advertising. Leveraging people's emotions to get them to buy more, to use more, while shaping values of superficiality is not what I want to do. People will never be fulfilled as we've promised by using these products; they will just need to have more, and buy more in the attempt to fill "the hole." There are certain categories of products, like beer and cosmetics, that I choose not to work on.
>
> On the other hand, I do feel okay about other things that I market. Selling care of the environment is good; selling health, tourism, art, fitness, spirituality is good. I feel good about selling these "products" because the "consumer promise" we are providing is true. If you help clean the environment, you can save the planet; if you exercise you will feel better; if you stay close to God your deepest need will be answered. These are not empty promises; they are the truth, and I feel good about telling the truth, about not manipulating others and creating a world of false truths or inappropriate values.

The struggle between the true Self and false self plays itself out within individuals and whole industries. The false self system does not have the same kind of independent identity that ego and Self do. It is a parasite that, once introduced into the stream of egoic consciousness, will spread throughout the system and infect every perception, decision, and behavior. To the extent that ego is persuaded that this way lies life, it is co-opted and becomes an obedient servant in the realm of the false self. But just as ego lost awareness of its connection with Self, it can work to recover that awareness and become once again the conscious agent of Self.

Fortunately, ego continues to emanate in every moment from its source in Self, even when much of its energy has been siphoned off into the false self system. As long as the tiniest spark of ego emanating from Self remains free, there is an individual consciousness that can be strengthened and reinforced to do battle with the false self in order to deconstruct the concrete pillbox existence it has built around itself for its own safety and security.

Suffering: The Safe-Cracker

One of the most effective means of reawakening the ego-Self connection is human suffering, generally brought on by the loss of people or things that had taken over our identity. Suffering is the hammer and chisel that effectively cracks open the safe of the false self system and reveals its counterfeit holdings. This is the point of departure for Buddhist spirituality. It begins with the recognition that life is suffering, and that the root of suffering is desire—understood as desires that emanate from the false self system. It invites one to reduce one's suffering by reducing one's (false self) desires.

Many other means are proposed by the spiritual life for awakening us to the reality that there is more to who we are in particular and more to life in general than responding to our false self desires for security, esteem, and control. But often we cannot find motivation to learn to meditate, volunteer in community service, engage in intercessory forms of prayer for others, keep a personal journal, do yoga or Tai Chi, or get out into nature to recover a sense of wholeness—until our world falls apart. Suddenly, we are motivated to give a critical examination to the system around which we have built our life.

It is for this reason that the cross is the symbol of Christianity: Suffering can be the carrier of meaning. It can be part of the process of new birth.

Merton effectively summarizes the perspectives laid out above:

> All sin starts from the assumption that my false self, the self that exists only in my own egocentric desires, is the fundamental reality of life to which everything else in the universe is ordered. Thus I use up my life in the desire for pleasures and the thirst for experiences, for power, honor, knowledge and love, to clothe this false self and construct its nothingness into something objectively real. And I wind experiences around myself and cover myself with pleasures and glory like bandages in order to make myself perceptible to myself and to the world....
>
> But there is no substance under the things with which I am clothed. I am hollow, and my structure of pleasures and ambitions has no foundation. I am objectified in them. But they are all destined by their very contingency to be destroyed. And when they are gone there will be nothing

left of me but my own nakedness and emptiness and hollowness, to tell me that I am my own mistake.[9]

To recapitulate: The Self is the subject of the unconscious, and ego is the subject of conscious experience, intellectual activity, and desire. They should not be related to as two *different subjects*, but as *two different experiences of who "I" am*. Self is "I" as the human spirit, present in all manner of experiences; ego is the conscious and active dimension of "I" in this embodied state. The false self system occurs when ego is infected by earlier emotional programming that influences decisions and behavior. Its "lock" on the ego can and must be broken if we are to discover who we really are and what our purpose is.

When Jesus talked about being set free to love, he said, "Truly, Truly, I say to you, unless the grain of wheat falls into the ground and dies, it remains alone; but if it dies, it bears much fruit. Whoever loves their life, loses it; whoever hates their life in this world, will keep it for eternal life" (John 12:24–25 RSV). The life to be lost is that of the false self, and eternal life is not just that life which begins after death, but the life that we are called to live *now* in the freedom of love.[10]

The biblical story of Tobit leaves no doubt in the mind as to what this freedom looks like. Tobit was among those many people taken into exile after the collapse of the Northern Kingdom of Israel some eight centuries before the birth of Jesus. But, like so many others, Tobit prospered in his new city, Nineveh. He served as a sort of purchasing agent for the royal household, a position that often required him to travel.

Tobit was a loyal Israelite. He spent much of his time doing good deeds, among them burying the bodies of fellow Israelites executed by the state. After an informer alerted the authorities that he was doing this, Tobit had to go into hiding for awhile. But within two months, through the efforts of a friend in court, Tobit was able to return home. With the table richly laid with an abundance of food for the feast of Pentecost, Tobit, true to character, sends his son Tobias out into the streets to invite someone less fortunate to dine with them. But the son returns with shocking news. The story unfolds, in Tobit's words:

> So Tobias went to look for some poor person of our people. When he had returned he said, "Father! One of our own people has been murdered and thrown into the market place and now he lies there strangled." Then I sprang up, left the dinner before even tasting it, and removed the body from the square and laid it in one of the rooms until sunset when I might bury it....When the sun had set, I went and dug the grave and buried him. And my neighbors laughed and said, "Is he still not afraid? He has already been hunted down to be put to death for doing this, and he ran away; yet here he is again burying the dead! (Tobit 2:3–5, 7, 8)

He may have been afraid, but his fear did not rule him. Tobit was free. He responded to a deeper, higher law, the law of love and compassion.

We set out on the road to freedom when we no longer let the fears and desires of the false self govern us. As we begin to put relationships, compassion, justice, and the service of others above our own needs for the esteem of others, acceptance, and security, the zone of spiritual freedom expands within.

4
Made for Communion

The spiritual life finds its fulfillment in bringing our entire life into a transforming, loving communion with God. This communion finds its first expression in the very existence of the Self. We become more and more conscious of this ineffable mystery at the root of our being through Self's communication with ego. The more that ego comes into alignment with Self, the more we consciously realize that our life simply makes no sense if it is not lived as the fruition of the communion with God that characterizes our deepest being. We were made for communion, and each one of us *is* a communion with God.

This explains, I believe, why Merton was always very careful in talking about the role of disciplines and methods in the spiritual life. In his purview, they are all just means to conscious communion, means to produce within ourselves something of the silence, the humility, the detachment, the purity of heart that are required if the Self is to make some subtle, unpredictable manifestation of its presence.

We should not look for a "method" or "system," but cultivate an "attitude," an "outlook": faith, openness, attention, reverence, expectation, supplication, trust, joy. All these finally permeate our being with love in so far as our living faith tells us we are in the presence of God, that we live in

Christ, that in the Spirit of God we "see" God our Father without "seeing." We know him in "unknowing."[1]

To the question, "Who am I?" Merton's response was "I am one loved by Christ," for it is Christ's love for us that establishes the Self in its true reality. He was clear in his own mind about our created nature remaining distinct from God when speaking of this mystical union.

> Even when the soul is mystically united with God there remains, according to Christian theology, a distinction between the nature of the soul and the nature of God. Their perfect unity is not then a fusion of natures, but a unity of love and experience.[2]

"God is love," writes John (1 John 4:8), so here is where we will find what it means to be like God. By our love and our need for love we call forth the Self, the habitat of God, in one another. The best thing we can do is to be who we are in God and to open ourselves to God's life in us. Then we will at once see ourselves and God in a unity of divine love. This experience of communion can be lived anywhere, in every form of activity. Our union with God is our Self, not any *thing* we know or do. When, through the deconstruction of the false self, this identity comes to light, we can say with Jacob, "Surely the Lord is in this place—and I did not know it! How awesome is this place! This is none other than the house of God and the gate of heaven" (Gen 28:17). Our whole spiritual life is this opening of ourselves to be existentially and consciously fulfilled by the communion with God that constitutes our own deepest reality.[3]

The Universe as a Communion Experience

This theme of communion is much more pervasive than we ever dreamed. One of the great discoveries of modern science is that the universe is differentiated. It has different centers, and everything is in communion with everything else. The whole universe, we are discovering, is a communion experience—a multiplicity of centers in communion with one another. Subjectivity, differentiation, communion are the laws of the fundamental order of the universe. The universe consists of subjects (everything has an "inside," an inner reality). These subjects are differentiated from each other, yet everything is an illustration of all three laws because the universe is a communion experience of a multiplicity of sentient beings. As Albert North Whitehead put it, "You can't catch the universe sleeping."[4] The universe is in communion with itself at every level of its being.

All of this causes geophysicist Brian Swimme to postulate that each of us is given a certain quantum energy and we have one essential task: to identify who we are. From that flows a second: to consciously *be* who we are. It is a task that demands tremendous strength and courage, because it involves differentiation. Each of us is someone who has never existed before and who will never exist again. Our value is in our difference. When we act from that difference, we make the greatest contribution we can make. In fact, only this differentiation will enable communion. The ultimate aim of the universe, says Swimme, is for each thing to be recognized for what it is in its sacred depth. The desire we have to create comes from the ultimate drive of the universe to differentiate in subjectivity and find communion.[5]

When we speak about the sacred depth of all things, we are recognizing God's presence as the Ground of all being. Because God is everywhere, we do not need to leave the place where we are and seek God's presence somewhere else. Once we have realized that what we seek is already given, any person, event, film, book, tree, flower, or circumstance of our life can speak to us of this mysterious communion at the source of our being. I used to go on retreat very focused on the preacher and carefully choosing one or two books on the spiritual life, looking for and wanting an insight. Now I usually just go apart for a week of silence and solitude in a beautiful place. I bring along my hiking shoes, swim trunks or cross-country skis, a few books, maybe some audiocassettes, my journal, and most important of all, an attitude of relaxed openness and attentiveness in faith, ready to use all of these instruments or none of them, aware that God can stir my heart through anything at anytime.

One of the stories that illustrates God's capacity to reach us through any means at all is found in the life of St. Augustine. While sitting in the garden outside, he heard two children playing a game. In the game, they repeatedly said to one another, *"tolle, lege; tolle, lege"* (take up and read). As he listened to their play, Augustine's eyes fell upon a Bible. He had been intending to take it up and read what it had to say, but had been inwardly resisting it. Now, in the voices of these children, Augustine heard God inviting him to "take and read." He did, and it was a moment of conversion for him. He went on to become one of the greatest teachers in the history of the church. The turning point for Augustine came through the voices of children playing outside his window.

When we are attentive and expectant in faith, God can use *anything* to touch our hearts and transform us, to bring us to the insight that we *are* the insight. There is no insight other than the Self—the habitat of God—we have always been, yet did not recognize. This is one of Merton's recurring emphases:

> If you descend into the depths of your own spirit...and arrive somewhere at the center of what you are, you are confronted with the inescapable truth that, at the very roots of your existence, you are in constant and immediate and inescapable contact with the Infinite power of God.[6]

Our peace and happiness depend on making this discovery. If we find God we will find our Self, and if we find our Self we will find God. Whatever we do, every act, however small, can teach us everything we need to know.[7]

Grace as God's Personal Self-Communication

Karl Rahner, one of the principal Catholic theologians of the twentieth century, speaks about every single human being as an "event" of the free self-communication of God. In other words, God is forever and always communicating God's self to us in ways that are liberating and unmerited and forgiving. Most of us learned to think about grace as a gift of God. But the greatest gift that God can give is the gift of God's very self. Rahner and other theologians speak of grace as "God's personal self-communication."

Grace, then, is not so much some *thing* that is given but *someone* who is experienced as present. This is why many theologians today do not speak so much of sacraments "giving grace" as of sacramental celebrations that enable us to *experience*

God's presence, to touch grace itself, to contact the all-pervading presence of the loving God who sustains all created things in existence. The sacraments allow us to become conscious and aware of God's greatest gift: the creative, sustaining, loving presence of God at the point of connection with Self.

In stressing this conviction of faith, it is important to hold onto the point made earlier in response to the question: Is God identical with or distinct from the Self? The answer of Christian faith is: both. The doctrine of "participation" in the energies of God, come to fullest expression in the Christian East, appeals to the metaphor of "sharing in" the divine being. The Self participates in the being of God, while at the same time remaining distinct from God. The Self has no reality apart from God, but neither is it identical with God. By extension, we can say that at every moment and in every place, everything created is both one in God and simultaneously distinct from God. As the communication among God, Self, and Ego becomes clearer, this truth is known experientially. Only then do we know what it means to live life to the full.

Am I To Let Go of Ego?

Self tells us both *that* we are and *who* we are. But Self is never found apart from individuals. Ego is the way Self comes to individual, personal consciousness. Without it, the potentiality of Self cannot be developed and expressed. Ego therefore has an important role to play. It should not be bad-mouthed or have its reputation smeared. If Self is the intelligent agent who runs the business in the back room, ego is the store-front manager. The contribution of both is needed to make the business go.

Ego needs to recognize that when it comes to vision statement and nature and purpose directives for the project, it is Self who will handle it. Ego's employment stems from an intelligence greater than itself. As long as there is good communication between the back room and the counter out front, the business flourishes. But when the lines of communication get jammed and ego starts running the store based on the advice it receives from interested parties (false self) at the counter, there are problems.

Nonetheless, ego has some important tasks to carry out and some decisions to make. It needs to have a good sense of itself and its role in things, hold regular consultation with Self about the matters it is facing, and be ready to make referrals when it is out of its depth. It needs to be ready to defer and submit, in short, to be passed over in certain questions. So are we to let go of it, annihilate it, deconstruct it? No. We must give it a good healthy sense of its place in the scheme of things, an accurate sense of who it is for others and the world. As Karlfried Graf Dürckheim says, "Humility is not wanting to appear more than one is, but it is also not wanting to appear less than one is, and in particular, less than that which one is in 'one's very being' and which one experiences."[8]

Ego's role is to become as authentic as it can, to become as honest, self-accepting, aware, and humble (grounded in truth) as possible. There are many ways in which ego can do this work, for example, through journaling, counseling, practicing honesty in speech, learning how to effectively and respectfully communicate feelings, acting according to personal conviction, using various personality inventory tools to foster self-awareness, employing a daily examination of consciousness, inviting feedback from others, participating in community. These various disciplines and programs are for life, because authentic living is not something that is ever finished. It is easy for us to slip off-center and fall back into the influence of the false self and the feel-good, illusory wares that it is always peddling.[9]

The false self is always ready to infect ego; it is always ready to inflate the value of its wares until they all seem to be stainless steel with a lifetime guarantee. When they begin to chip and stain, however, disillusionment can be great and sometimes have tragic consequences. I once knew a salesman who had been having a difficult first half of the year, but who had nevertheless made several sales in the previous month, which enabled him and his partner to almost erase their debts. He had been in a severe depression for the last several weeks of the year, and on New Year's Eve he drove out of town with a shotgun in the car, pulled off to the side of the road, and squeezed the trigger.

One of the stories that surfaced in the aftermath was that he had expressed concern to his wife about his thinning hair. As a salesman, he felt he needed to maintain a good image. So he investigated hair transplants. The price tag was hefty—about $10,000. His wife indicated that she thought the money would be better put either toward their own future or their children's education, but that she would support him if he really wanted to spend it this way.

He had the transplant work done, and then became very self-conscious about it, even to the point of not wanting to go out for fear of what people would think of him. The phrase he used was, "I am afraid that people will discover the deceit of my life." In the note he left his wife and children, he wrote: "I can simply no longer cope with the problems I have brought upon myself."

It would be false to this man to suggest that his decision to proceed with the hair transplant fully explains an act like suicide and the deep and pervasive suffering from which it springs. We can only observe, fully aware of our inability to grasp the suffering of the other, the profound psychic wounds that the false self desperately tries to protect, and how the ego struggles to be in contact with the Self and sometimes succumbs to discouragement and despair.

The false self offers ego an answer to its yearning, but the solution is nowhere deep enough. Yet those yearnings for security, esteem, power are so incessant and their appetite so insatiable, that just discovering who we really are and being content to be that is a life-work. We are all participants in the struggle to be authentic. It's just a question of where we are on the spectrum at any point in time. The story of this man is a tragic, modern parable of the emptiness we reap when we base our sense of ourselves on how other people perceive us, when we stake our savings on our "image." The difference between the false self and the true Self requires constant discernment. We ignore the infinite difference between the two at our own risk and peril.

The Great Relief

"Come to me," Jesus calls to those who can hear, "all you who labor and are heavy burdened, and I will give you rest" (Matt 11:28). We don't have to give up our false-self adherence as if it were a bad habit, something we "ought not to do." We simply drop it because we've found out it's a poor investment with a small chance of any real return. Awareness is the catalyst. Once we see its counterfeit nature, we stop investing, because we've found out it isn't true. It's not authentic. "You will know the truth, and the truth will make you free" (John 8:32).

"So come to me and get relief," Jesus says. And the Great Relief is dropping the false self. "Come to me and identify with me rather than with those superficial identities which are all relative and subject to change. I am the Reality beyond all the unstable ego identifications, roles, and judgments. I am the Way and the Truth and the Life."[10]

Craig is a college professor, much loved by his students and colleagues. As I have watched him over the years, he has become increasingly more at home in his skin and at peace with the world. His story illustrates how, once the false self's cover is blown and we get a look at the vaudeville act the wizard is running behind the curtain of the ego, our perception changes toward what the false self offers and our identity with it weakens.

> It had been approximately three years since my return to religious practice. I had spent the preceding twenty living a life centered on enjoyment—the easy life, entertainment, travel to exotic destinations, a pleasant committed relationship, and all those other quests subtly imposed by the media culture. However, during all this period I was subjected to a soft but firm compulsion for sexual pleasure. It never drew me into trouble of any kind—relational, legal, professional or other, but constantly colored my view of things, and took an undue amount of space in my decision-making. There were occasional infidelities, seemingly harmless, since my partner was unaware—never serious, however, never lasting more than a few hours, days, weeks,

often linked to foreign destinations, out of reach for anyone in my immediate environment and shrouded in caution and discretion. And all of that seemed quite normal.

Prior to that phase of my life, I had been a "good boy," sincere in my search for God to the extent of engaging in several years of theological studies as a lay person to better nourish the quest. All that had come to a grinding halt with the realization of my homosexuality. I had finally admitted this to myself and in that context ardently wished to be united with another in a relationship of mutual dedication in committed love. I became quite comfortable with assuming this facet of my identity and learned to be who I was, respectful of myself and of those around me, whom I gently invited to live the joy of my new freedom. But the wagging finger of my Church came between me and my God. The God incarnate in my Church refused the likes of me. I remember, still with deep emotion, the quiet moment in an empty church when I spilled the pain of my rejection to God and like a chided lover took painful leave of Him. "Call me when you speak a language I can understand, but not before! I am who I am and it seems you want nothing of me! I don't understand; I thought you were a loving God!"

Well, God did wait for a tender spot to open in my heart. He pursued me tenderly, stalked me lovingly. And finally, having felt His discrete but obstinate presence I looked back, behind my shoulder. And there He stood ever so gently. I opened up slightly, cautiously, and progressively let Him in. I experienced the deep peace of reconciliation with myself, with God and recovered a level of quiet peace which had gradually oozed out of my life. Enjoyment was being replaced by joy, the conformity of non-conformity by autonomy, living out of the superficial by tapping into the real.

After the proverbial honeymoon with my long-lost Lover and the difficult adjustment of my everyday life to my new commitment to a God re-found, the reality of my sexual obsession slowly surfaced through my newfound serenity. The weeds were beginning to choke the newly budding flowers. Living my fidelity to God became a growing challenge, and somehow I was increasingly losing the battle. I had opted with my life companion to live in abstinent chastity, but somehow the trouble was coming from elsewhere, less from the exterior than from interior demons. I prayed as I never prayed before, invoking every saint from Christ himself to the friend whose funeral I last attended. But somehow, nothing was happening. Was God once again letting me down?

At this point in the relationship, I knew I could only desperately trust. That somewhere on the way that same God who had pursued me for twenty years was somehow inviting me to journey further on. I couldn't see, couldn't understand! Childlike loving trust was my only anchor. The pleasurable consolation of God had all but disappeared—prayer was dry and seemingly meaningless. I repeatedly fell, maybe less frequently than before, but none-the-less hard. The difference however, resided in the fact that now I had unflinching hope, hope in a God I trusted absolutely because He had been constantly by my side.

Then one day, quite by accident, I learned of someone who had had some experience in diverse twelve-step movements, among them Sexaholics Anonymous. Deep down, I felt the gentle, loving, teasing smile of God. But all of that remained deep mystery: what was this about, how did it fit, where was it going? Resting in that confidence, I maneuvered my way to meeting this person if only to put my hands on a telephone number which I could call to investigate this avenue which was opening in my life.

Three weeks later, I had made contact with SA and come to the realization that I was a sex addict, a sexaholic! It was a deep, traumatic recognition, one which had the potential of luring me into the almost hopeless despair of shame. But I almost immediately understood in my heart that I was possibly holding the key to inner freedom. I could put a name to what I was living so painfully, I could look it straight in the eyes, it was out of the shadows.

And I can still remember my repugnance at opening the door into the meeting room for my first meeting. What? Me? A sexaholic? That's fine for me to admit to myself, but to face others as a sexaholic? The pain! But somehow I felt almost physically the gentle hand of God, almost like that of a parent lovingly sheltering a child on the walk to school the first day of kindergarten. And so I went in, and I realized I was home, with the most beautiful collection of people I had ever met—humble, true, transparent, and radiant in their illness. I deeply experienced the unfathomable love of God. I resolved to live just who I was, in whatever way He taught me through this motley crew... and I was one of them!

The journey has been rough but seasoned none-the-less with ever-deepening joy! The process is one of acceptance, of crude, true, unabashed realism in the vision of who I am. There has been the occasional slip, but so many more victories. And every victory has been that of a God who lives so intimately within, whom I can only see through those without—my brothers and sisters in the movement, my sponsors, those with whom I am journeying to fundamental truth. My slips! Moments where I have relied on my strength. I know that my increasing power is in my maturing awareness of my weakness. God is becoming more and more essential through a constantly growing awareness of His presence in my life. Living for a fleeting future is giving way to savoring the moment.

And yes! I think I can now understand the joy of a Mary Magdalen who in her social destitution experienced the deep enveloping love of the God who came to her in her seemingly senseless journey. In fact, I rather think that the shame she experienced in marginality must have given way to a beautiful sense of pride—that of being deeply, personally loved and chosen for what she was by Christ, by Love Himself.

On my return from a brief period of absence from my home group in Sexaholics Anonymous, I was told that we had to find a new place to meet. We were now to get together in a new institution. My reaction was swift and somewhat frightened. Without my knowledge we had moved to a house where several people knew me. Could they, and would they deduct that I also was a sexaholic or identify me as one? I must say that I'd be proud to stand up as myself, truly loved by God, truly grateful, and beaming from the joy of resting in Him.

But more importantly, I have become thankful for my addiction—I'm a happy addict! I will be an addict for the rest of my life. But the catch is that my addiction has become a channel of grace. I have at last found God in my truth, my weakness. And my weakness has been the fertile soil of His loving strength. My love affair with God is but beginning, and I know it will never end. I am so thankful for my illness, for living it in its deepest truth, for it is restoring my relationship with God.

Dismantling the False Self

The false self lives out of a siege mentality and thrives on the motivation of *fear*. It comes up through the trap door of our life experience around issues of survival/security, affection/esteem, power/control.

It would be impossible to exaggerate, for example, the amount of attention and affection that an infant needs in order to feel secure. It is precisely that feeling of security that enables the emotional life of the child to unfold in a healthy way. But suppose the child is born into an environment in which one of the parents has a drug addiction and the other is seldom there. The child's needs are often unattended to, and he breathes in an air of insecurity. It is not likely that this child as it grows up will step forward with confidence and energy to meet the challenges of life. Deprived of security, the particular security symbols of the culture he grows up in will exert a powerful attraction and he will probably not be aware of why it is so important for him to have that house or car or a full refrigerator.

Or suppose that a young woman grows up in a part of the world where opportunities for a good education and a decent job are scarce, in short, where there is little power and control over one's future. Then, by some good fortune she gets a scholarship opportunity that takes her to another country where a world of new possibilities now present themselves. The emotional need for control over her life becomes a strong center of motivation. If she does not become aware of that need and consciously guide its expression, she may end up trying to control every situation and every person.

In Thomas Keating's words, "The false self is the syndrome of our emotional programs for happiness grown into sources of motivation and made much more complex by the socialization process, and reinforced by our over-identification with our cultural conditioning. Our ordinary thoughts, reactions and feelings manifest the false self on every level of our conduct."[11]

The heart of the problem, Keating notes, is *to change the direction in which we are looking for happiness.* And that means addressing the unconscious motivations that are still in place and directing our lives. Failure to do this explains why, even after we have had a conversion experience, enthusiasm wanes after a year or two, and when the former temptations recur, we fall back into the old destructive patterns of living. Earlier manuals on the life of the soul spoke of "spiritual combat"; it is impossible to avoid when what we want to do squares off with what we feel we should do. And the struggle will not be over quickly. We see that we are dealing with subtle forces that are powerful and fully in place. To dismantle these value systems in favor of the values of the gospel is not a matter of a week-long retreat. Spiritual highs provide some temporary relief, but when their tranquilizing effect wears off, we feel the pain of our dissatisfaction recurring with full force if we have not addressed their underlying causes.[12]

We can read book after book on the spiritual life, but if we do not have a practice that attacks these false-self energy centers, we will make little progress. The undigested emotional material of early childhood is stored in the body and nervous system, hindering the free flow of grace, preventing us from living in the here and now, and keeping us so preoccupied with meeting our own needs that we are incapable of serving the needs of others.

We need to name the emotional response that is repeating itself and then identify the event from which it originates. What remains after that is to dismantle the false self system by letting go of its concrete manifestations in daily life. When we become aware that an emotional response is operating, we name it and say to ourselves, "I give up my demand for security (or control or esteem)." Notice it. Name it. Deny it.

Let's say that you and your friend are going out to a movie. You've both looked at the movie listings in the paper to see what attracted you, but put off making the final decision until meeting for supper beforehand. When the time comes, your friend's first choice is different from yours. She wanted the comedy and you preferred the emotional love story. No problem! You spot your inclination for control, name it to yourself, and respond, "No, we're going to see the film she wants to see." And in the meantime you increase your inner space of freedom, widen your range of pleasure. You thought only the love story could bring you satisfaction, and you returned home feeling that some good belly laughs were the best thing for you.

Each time we spot one of the false self's warning flares—that if we don't say this or do that, we may not get the security, control, or affirmation desired—and we decide to ignore the flare and follow our own inner radar indicating what would be honest or authentic for us to do or say in this situation, we are calmly dismantling the false self's strategy for survival and writing a new one.

It may simply be a situation in which we come to the table so hungry that we're ready to dive into the bowl and start eating with our hands. The message sent out from the false self, always looking out for its own comfort and security, is: "Grab that casserole and get the biggest piece before someone else does! Nobody can be as hungry tonight as I am!" Then we suggest that the person at the other end of the table start the dish by serving herself.

The approach is one of taming, of calming the demands of the false self, of asking it to keep quiet, to remain in its place and not get all excited ("This is not a life-threatening situation; the other movie might be good, too"). The false self was formed from early experiences of deprivation; now that those needs are being met in healthy ways, it no longer needs to protect me. Ego can let it go gently and compassionately. Now that ego is in communication with the true Self and following its lead, the false self can fade out peacefully. The true Self, in fact, rather than violently blasting the false self out of the water with a warrior-like cry, will lie down with it in the image of Isaiah: "The wolf shall live with the lamb, the leopard shall lie down with the kid, the calf and the fatling and the lion together…and the weaned child shall put its hand on the adder's den. They will not hurt or destroy on all my holy mountain: for the earth will be full of the knowledge of the LORD" (Isa 11:6–9).

When Jesus goes from his baptism in the Jordan into the desert for forty days, he is clearly toning his spiritual energies through prayer and fasting in preparation for his mission. Notice how the temptations of the devil (Luke 4:1–13) during this time are precisely in the strongholds of the false self.

Survival/Security: "He ate nothing at all during those days, and when they were over he was famished. The devil said to him, 'If you are the Son of God, command this stone to become a loaf of bread.'"

Power/Control: "Then the devil led him up and showed him all the kingdoms of the world….'To you I will give their glory and all this authority….'"

Affection/Esteem: "If you are the Son of God, throw yourself down from here (the pinnacle of the Temple), for it is written: 'He will command his angels concerning you, to protect you, and on their hands they will bear you up….'"

But note, as well, that Jesus' strategy of response is to *notice* what Satan is doing ("Do not put the Lord your God to the test"), to *name* the positive behavior desired ("Worship the Lord your God and serve only him"), and to *deny* what Satan is offering ("One does not live by bread alone").

Then comes a nominee for the scariest line in the Bible: "When the devil had finished every test, he departed from him *until an opportune time*" (Luke 4:13, emphasis mine). Our spiritual freedom from the wiles of the enemy exploiting our points of greatest vulnerability is a constantly growing thing, and every gain must be consolidated and defended again and again. A definitive victory can never be declared. The distance gained from the deep-seated motivational patterns of the false self must be won and rewon. Constant vigilance is required. The enemy will be back at "an opportune time," and in that next encounter our spiritual freedom will either grow or be diminished.

5

Becoming Free

In experimenting with practical ways to expand the field of inner freedom, I discovered quite by accident a veritable oil well of possibility. When I turned fifty I decided to lead a retreat week-end that ended in a big birthday party. I chose the retreat theme "Savoring Life by Facing Our Mortality". Friends and family came in from far and wide, not fully aware in some cases what they were getting into. But everybody eventually tuned in, and it turned out to be a powerful experience.

Once I got into working with this theme of facing our mortality I saw what an effective way it offers of dismantling the false-self system. As a matter of fact, I found it to be so life-giving that I led several similar retreat weekends in the years to follow, and have now expanded it into a week-long retreat. I felt that more "digestive" and reflection time in between the sessions would enable the participants to do deeper and more enduring inner work.

There is very little in our culture that supports our facing our mortality; there is a great deal that is ready to distract us from it or try to convince us that it's all just a big illusion, that we can stay young and well forever if we just eat right and exercise enough and stay out of the sun. Even before I led that first week-end, I had an intuition that allowing the inevitability of our death to penetrate our consciousness would have the very salutary effect of sending us back to life with deeper gratitude for the gift given and sharpen the edge of our desire to live it fully. That is exactly what it proved to do. When we truly *realize* that this precious commodity called life-on-earth is given in limited supply, we savor it all the more. I am the greatest beneficiary of these retreats, and I truly love working with this theme. It is not about death; it is about *life and freedom*.

Obviously, *death* is one word that the false self erases from the dictionary. It is declared *verboten* in all conversation. The reason is simple: Death is the foil to the false self's fool-proof plan of providing security, affection, and control *forever*.

In these retreats, I walk the participants through the teaching of all the world religions on death and underline their common wisdom: The best way to dismantle your fear around death is to begin practicing for it now. To begin anticipating it in little tastes. This is called "spiritual dying." It doesn't have anything to do with losing one's faith or one's sense of the sacred. It just means to begin consciously entering into and practicing "letting go" each day. Death is the Big and Final Letting-Go, the grand finale as it were, and each day offers us several dress rehearsals. If we learn to befriend this experience, to unmask it, we see that it is not as horrendous as it is cracked up to be, and our fear around it begins to dissolve. Or even if everything we are afraid of does come to pass, we see that it wasn't as fierce as feared. What's more, we begin to see that from every experience of "dying" to some preference or desire, some new life issues forth. The freedom within us grows. What had before enslaved us out of fear no longer does because we experience for ourselves that the terrible losses predicted are really quite sustainable. Death, we discover, is highly overrated and ultimately safe.

Working with the notion of "spiritual dying" is just one of the ways in which we can actively and consciously participate in the deconstruction of the false-self system. Each night before I go to bed, I ask myself, "How did I practice for my death today? What 'like' or 'preference' did I let go of? What clamoring 'need' did I look at squarely in the eye and then step back from? Where did I put the needs of another before my own?"

Spiritual Freedom

"For freedom Christ has set us free. Stand firm, therefore, and do not submit again to a yoke of slavery" (Gal 5:1). The spiritual life leads to freedom. The important question, Merton said, is not "Am I happy?" but "Am I free?" Free to choose what I most deeply want to do. "As servants of God, live as free people, but do not use your freedom for evil," wrote the apostle Peter (1 Pet 2:16). In Merton's view, if I am really free to choose, I will do the things God wants me to do. Freedom is both *from* and *for*. Freedom *from* the net of many strings and expectations the false self has created. Freedom *from* the fear that if I step out of that particular role, I will disappoint someone. Freedom *from* the fear that if I do not espouse position "x" I will not be accepted.

Freedom *for* relates to positive and collaborative action in working with God to concretize the dream God has for the world and its inhabitants. A friend in Washington, D.C., who has founded a low-rent housing corporation to give poor people some constructive options constantly reminds me that "most of this holistic spirituality and contemplative prayer stuff doesn't speak to the lower-income people and their neighborhoods. It's generally pretty individualistic and doesn't connect with the poor or have much time for the social gospel. Wellness centers are usually in places where people have the money to pay and they never have anything to do with politics and social change." Such criticisms must influence the use of our freedom *for*. Love of God that does not show itself in service to humankind is a snare and a delusion.

For the Christian, the transformation of ego from "me-consciousness" to God-consciousness passes by Jesus. He is God's anointed one. How God is, we find in Jesus. At some point, it is not enough for ego to say that it is pursuing wholeness. The vision the false self gives us of what has lasting value and significance needs to be replaced by the vision that God gives us in Christ. Shifting our point of reference from the false self to the Self is referred to in Christian faith as the process of conversion. It is not a snapshot, done in a flash and then laminated to last a lifetime. It is a film, and the camera is always rolling. It relates to allowing our daily life experience in all the roles we play and identifications we carry and judgments we make to be shaped and guided by our true Self. We are thus always standing with one foot at the center of our interior life (Self) and one foot at the periphery (ego) where we interface with the world.

Our process of conversion will be complete when we have allowed Christ to reside in us so fully that it is *his* presence, *his* love, and *his* power that others encounter in our presence. Elizabeth-Anne Vanek describes how she has come to understand conversion:

> What this means in terms of loving is that my real task is to surrender to that inner presence which is Love Incarnate. Instead of hoping that those I encounter experience me as a compassionate person, I hope instead that they experience

Christ's compassionate presence through me. Instead of hoping that those with whom I work recognize my skills as a healer of the spirit, I hope instead that they experience the skills of Christ the healer. Instead of hoping that others find motivation and energy through *my* charisma, through *my* creativity, I hope instead that they see beyond my gifts, to the presence of the indwelling God. To become Love, then, is nothing less than to allow Christ to reside at the center of self.[1]

In her book *From Center to Circumference*, Vanek recounts how, in the past, she had given much thought as to how to make God the center of her life. She had worked on stripping herself of ego attachments to allow God more room. It seemed, however, that she was being called to a deeper relationship than this. In her imagination, she saw herself as a circle with God as a dot in the center.

> Gradually, the dot began to expand, losing its clearly defined boundaries, merging with the rest of the circle until center and circumference became one. The new call was for God to be both center and circumference; the new call was for God to become the totality of myself, so that it was indeed God who lived in me and I in God.[2]

She relates how, as she began responding to this new call, she began to lose all sense of the jumbled wants, needs, fears, resentments, and disappointments that had formerly constructed her "I," her false-self ego.

In my newness, I saw things differently, heard things differently and felt differently. All my senses seemed to be heightened, my way of knowing had become more encompassing, my capacity for compassion had intensified, my creativity was exploding....I could no longer define myself by my various roles—by what I *did*—but only by what I had become. I could no longer think of future in terms of "goals," "strategies" and "security," but only as it related to the unfolding of God's dream for me. I could no longer approach life as a limited opportunity for exercising my gifts, but instead found myself passionately committed to empowering others. No longer ruled by attachments, I experienced an incredible sense of liberation—a holy indifference as to whom I did (or did not) impress, as to what I did (or did not) accomplish, as to what I did (or did not) own.

...Physically I looked the same, but the essence of my true self (which I name the Christ-self) shone through. Instead of reaching out to a transcendent God, I found God residing fully in the center of myself.[3]

She goes on to recognize that this peeling away of the false self is not a once-in-a-lifetime event, but a continuing reality; she recognizes that, as much as she would like to just move into a permanent state of conscious union with the Divine, she has "unfinished business" to grapple with, memories that still scar the psyche, issues that still derail her emotionally. But she is committed to the demasking of the false self until only the Christ-self is left. "Now I live, not I, but Christ lives in me" (Gal 2:20).

The whole idea of allowing one's own "I" or ego to be superceded by another's may be particularly difficult for those who have little positive sense of themselves, whose ego is weak, bruised, or battered. Some women, for example, have nothing to give up, nothing to freely surrender because it has been taken from them by abusive men. The language of humility, of sur-render, of giving up power, of giving oneself over, doesn't work when the issues are about *reclaiming* a sense of self and power in a healthy way. There is no substitute in the spiritual journey for first developing a healthy and wholesome sense of oneself in the world. One has to first have a good ego before it can be freely and positively offered in a self-transcending act.

Freedom Is Not Elimination But Awareness and Integration

When a healthy sense of ourselves is present, we can enter into talk about self-gift, about entering into communion with God, about "the dot gradually expanding, losing its clearly defined boundaries, merging with the rest of the circle until cen-ter and circumference become one," about "God becoming the totality of myself, so that it was indeed God who lived in me and I in God."

If we are really serious about this inner work and turn our lives over to Christ, life will never be predictable again. Things we have taken for granted will become strangely insignificant. Goals we have pursued lose their meaning. Relations that were once so important to us seem frivolous. The more the gospel takes root in our hearts, the more that dot starts moving out toward the circumference. Decisions about how we spend time and money, where we worship, how we earn our living, what we eat, and how much we own are choices now made in the light of the gospel. And in so doing, we may begin to separate ourselves from friends, family, and much of the surrounding society. Higher consciousness has its price. Our growth in awareness often leads to changes in attitude and behavior. These changes can drive a wedge between friends, family, even spouses, and entail considerable suffering. "What is essential," writes Vanek, "is that we steadfastly hold to the belief that nothing is more important than our spiritual journey: any choice we make needs to be determined in light of our relationship with God."[4]

To leave behind the ego-centered, long-fought-for, and once-cherished worldly empire in order to follow the whispers coming from the inner depths of the Self is to embark upon a religious quest. It is to be like Abraham and Sarah, going in search of a new horizon at God's command. Like Abraham, we are asked to sacrifice our only child, our prized and cherished false self. And paradoxically, our willingness to do so enables the deed to be done without the death of the ego. The false self is the ram caught in the nearby thicket of desires and is put on the altar of sacrifice; but ego lives on as Isaac lived, not annihilated, but integrated into God's plan of action. Freedom is not elimination; it is awareness, knowledge, and integration.

The more that inspiration from God through Self informs and directs the activity of ego, the freer we become. Ego must continue to "play the game," to operate through the various roles and identifications that of necessity characterize its life. Self cannot manifest in the world without a concrete existence, without a visible agent. So there will be difficulties, praise, rejection, honors, mistakes, and criticism, but ego will carry them more lightly. The more ego sees the changeableness, the ephemeral character of its various roles and identifications, the less seriously it takes them, the less it invests in them, and the more it stays close to Self, living out of its wisdom and indestructibility and "oneing" with it as much as it can.

The fourteenth-century Dominican mystic and preacher Meister Eckhart spoke of the "core of the soul." This core, he tells us

> ...by nature...is sensitive to nothing but the divine Being, unmediated. Here God enters the soul with all he has and not in part. He enters the soul through its core and nothing may touch that core except God himself...In that core is the central silence [that allows] the utterance of God's word.[5]

Eckhart offers us here a description of the true Self as pure receptivity, alert and sensitive to the divine Presence. This Self is profoundly silent and undisturbed by the frenetic business of ego because its energy is focused on attending to the divine Presence. The passions, ideas, fears, ambitions, drives, habits, and attitudes of the ego surround it, but the Self remains tranquil and serene. It is the uncluttered ground that connects us with the source of our being, a quiveringly alert availability or "active repose" that enables us to listen and respond to the whispers of God.[6] It is a perpetual "Now,"

> ...unconscious of yesterday or the day before, and of tomorrow and the day after, for in eternity there is no yesterday nor any tomorrow, but only Now, as it was a thousand years ago and as it will be a thousand years hence, and is at this moment, and as it will be after death.[7]

Because the Self is permanently in the present, it is the place where Presence reveals itself. Since it is limited neither by the distractions of ego nor the blowing sands of time, it lives in unimpeded freedom. It resists conceptualization and classification, remaining pure and free, like God. It is that part of us most receptive to God, most real, reflecting God as absolute Reality and recognizing God's Spirit as kindred. The true Self knows that ego, my external persona turned toward everyday affairs, is not my true identity — it isn't that which, at the end of the day, grounds who and what I am. The spiritual life is a process of discovering the true Self and coming to dwell in it, to put down permanent roots in it and to become "at home" in it.[8]

As this conversion takes deeper and deeper hold, what Eckhart refers to as "agents of the soul" (thoughts, sensations, emotions), are gradually harnessed and put in the service of the Self. All the natural gifts, talents, and interests that characterize ego are subordinated to and draw direction from the Self. This in-gathering has an integrating and harmonizing effect. Our hitherto dispersed and self-absorbed ego opens to the call of the Self and rechannels its energies for the sake of the true Self. With time, the light at the core of the soul radiates out through the soul's agents, overflowing into the seamless garment of the body-mind. What was alienated is integrated. What was broken is healed. What was enslaved becomes free. Our entire being is ennobled by being suffused with that which is most noble within us. We become calm and tranquil dwellers, at home in and with ourselves, instead of aliens in a strange land.[9] We are becoming free.

Reflection Questions

A. Identify some experiences in your life where these three characteristics of who you are move out of the abstract and become real for you.

    Creature: vulnerable, dependent, needy, finite, fallible

    Sinner: one who strays, misses the mark, deviates, turns away

    Child of God: beloved of God, forgiven, accepted, blessed, nurtured, guided, chosen

B. Within your own present spiritual life, which of these motifs is the dominant one?

C. Can you think of an area of struggle in your life where inner freedom came, not through repression and elimination, but through awareness, knowledge/acceptance, and integration?

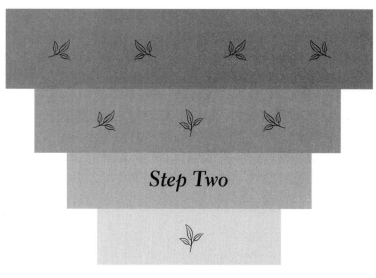

Step Two

Live Your Calling to the Full

Soul Fire

Throw open the door of that furnace
where the flames come leaping forth
like hungry hounds on the hunt,
licking and lapping at every cue on the trail
of the divine design for your life.
Ask not: where is it written?
It is written on your heart
in the colors of desire.
It is sung by the silent voices
of your recurring dreams.
It is the refrain chanted
by the chorus of your accumulating years:
"If not now, when? If not here, where?"
And the only obedience that will set you free is
                        surrender
to the energy and fire congealed in your gifts.

6

The Role of Desire
in Decision Making

Making a positive contribution to the world in which we live is the rent we pay for the space we occupy on the planet. Once we know who we are and ego and Self are in alignment, it is much easier to get the message of how God would like us to use our gifts for leaving this world better than we found it. I would describe the Christian calling in general as "availability for service in love." But how each one of us gives concrete expression to that general vocation will look very different from one person to another.

In Step Two toward spiritual freedom, we will focus on the experience of call and the questions that surround it: How do we know a call is from God? What are the signs by which to discern it? Where do we find sustenance when the going gets rough? What kind of a process of decision making results in a clear and unconflicted heart ready to respond to and fully live one's call? In reflecting on the experience of call, we will also consider some guidelines for discernment useful for general application in our effort to live our call fully.

Our starting point is human desire. How much weight should be given to the role of desire in the decisions we make? In her book *The Artist's Way: A Spiritual Path to Higher Creativity*, Julia Cameron writes, "What we really want to do is what we are really meant to do. When we do what we are meant to do, money comes to us, doors open for us, we feel useful, and the work we do feels like play to us."[1]

Thomas Merton's approach is more careful and qualified, but moves in the same direction: A real connection *frequently* exists between our spontaneous desires and God's will for us. In his view, our "holy and spiritual desires" do really "represent a possibility of a special, spontaneous and personal gift" that we alone can make to God. If such a gift is there, then surely God asks that gift from us. What is more, a "holy, humble, and sincere desire may be one of the signs that God asks it!"[2] In short: Our deep longings can be very important cues of God's will for us.

In the Spiritual Exercises, Ignatius of Loyola encourages the retreatant to ask for two things at the beginning of every prayer period: One begins by asking God for help; and one continues by asking God for "what I want and desire." Authentic desire tends to be rooted in the true Self. As we refer with greater and greater fidelity to the Self for guidance, we become increasingly aware of our authentic desires. Desire is the doorway through which the Divine enters. Praying at the heart of one's burning desires invites God into one's living space. Thus does Ignatius counsel one to begin every period of prayer by locating and enunciating one's deep desire.

Distinguishing between Authentic and Ephemeral Desires

A careful approach to the role of desire in making decisions to follow our call is warranted, however. All desires are real experiences, but they are not all equally authentic. Distinguishing between authentic and ephemeral desires involves a groping and fallible process because it is often difficult for us to know our deeper desires and to separate them out from the more superficial ones.[3]

What is the divining rod that will enable us to recognize the difference between the two? Jesuit psychologist Wilkie Au cites three helpful criteria.[4] First, authentic desires are integrally connected with who we are; they flow from the Self. An effective divining rod is the question: What do I want? I mean, what do I *really* want? This was the question that Jesus put to the first disciples in John's account of their call (John 1:35–39). He directed them to their deepest desires.

Second, the more authentic our desires, the more they will move us toward self-donation to God and others and away from self-centeredness. If ego is in close alignment with Self, the distinction between what "I" want and what God wants begins to blur. The deeper we reach into ourselves, the more we experience desires that are uniquely our own but which emanate from God and are God-given. In the exercise of testing and interpreting our desires, it is highly recommended to engage others who can provide some objectivity in the process. The potential for self-deception is always real. The false self is a con artist.

Third, as paradoxical as it may seem, authentic desires are always in some way public. That is to say, they stem from communal values, not just individual ones. They lead us out of ourselves and into the human community. For example, the desire to use our talents in service of others is more authentic than only using them for private gain because it reflects our true nature as social beings.

I have a friend who recently provided an example of what this kind of discernment looks like in flesh-and-blood application. Jim pastors a small, multidenominational Christian church in the inner city of Washington, D.C. He also serves as the chairman of Manna, Inc., a low-income housing and community development project. Jim helped found these two organizations twenty years ago in response to what he felt as God's call back then.

Recently, Jim was invited to consider becoming the executive director of a retreat center in his home state of Arkansas. Twenty-nine years earlier, he had picked up and left everything to answer a call in the District of Columbia. His original dream at that time was to go back to Arkansas one day and start a new church community, but he never made it. "Is God calling me again, once again," he wondered, "to leave everything and everyone I hold near and dear here and follow Jesus to a new land that he will show me?"

Jim invited some of his friends to "sit in" on his discernment process and to keep him honest in it. He realized that it was very tempting for him to settle in and enjoy the fruit of many years of labor. His children were close by and he delighted in relating to them at the young adult stage of their lives. He knew in his head, but struggled in his heart, with the realization that no matter whether we stay put or take off to other places, Jesus continually calls his disciples to leave everything that is temporary and follow him. He recognized that this earth and life is not our final home, nor the place to put down our full weight no matter how good it gets; that this life is transitional shelter, not permanent housing; that we are only sojourners and not permanent guests here. He preached this all the time to his people, but was finding it difficult to apply it to the decision he faced.

Jim needed to reconnect with his deepest desire. In sifting through his life history, he saw that one of the early turning points in his faith journey came through finding two books[5] about the Church of the Saviour community in Washington. "When I read them, I knew immediately this was what I wanted and needed for my survival and growth. The Church of the Saviour's call and commitment to integrate and practice the 'inward' (personal) and 'outward' (social) faith journey in the context of a committed, diverse Christian community was my call, too. I wanted to belong to a group of people who were willing to make significant commitments of support and accountability to one another as they sought to be faithful to Jesus' call on their lives."

In reflecting on this earlier experience, Jim came to see that his call has always involved building an alternative form of church and community across race and class lines whether in Little Rock, Arkansas, Washington, D.C., or anywhere else. "This is my home and the people are my good friends, coworkers, colleagues, and neighbors. Over the past thirty years my call has been refined by fire, clarified, deepened, and expanded, but it has not changed at the core," Jim said. "I'm probably more called to it now than ever before. I know that wherever I go or whatever I do in the future, I will be doing this in one form or another." That is the kind of statement that reflects our deepest desire. Locating what we *really* want to do responds to the first criteria for distinguishing between ephemeral and authentic desires.

It is clear that Jim's call moves him outward in self-donation to others and away from self-centeredness, the second criteria for distinguishing between authentic and ephemeral desires. Over the years, the stresses and pressures of his life and work in the inner city led him to expand his prayer life, the inward journey, by cultivating a more holistic and contemplative prayer practice. He works at weaving the social, political, and countercultural dimensions of his life, experienced in the outward journey, into his prayer. It was undoubtedly this amalgam of interests and abilities that made him an attractive candidate to run a retreat center.

But in his own discernment, Jim concluded that "I'm not called solely to specialize in teaching this holistic spiritual practice through conducting retreats, classes, special events, and programs. Personally living a more integrated and balanced life is only one aspect of a larger call: to establish a contemplative prayer practice at the heart of my church's life and to relate Christian contemplative prayer to the social and political dimensions of Jesus' gospel and spirituality." In saying as much, Jim named the third trait for identifying authentic desires: They are not just individual and private ones, but are always in some way public, stemming from communal values.

In the end, Jim felt that the will of God is written into our being at the point of our gifts, and one's call is best discerned by knowing and doing what one loves. "Do that which you cannot help doing, which you would do even when not paid for it," he said, quoting a Japanese proverb. While recognizing that the basic components of his call—to promote, teach, and practice a holistic approach to the inward and outward spiritual journey in Christian community—were exportable to any locale hungry for and receptive to it, he came to the conclusion that he wasn't called to leave the inner city nor to give up on developing an alternative form of the local church. Presently, he is experiencing the fruit of his faithfulness in this long and uncertain process in the form of some exciting breakthroughs and new developments in this new chapter of his life and work in the District.

Discernment and "God's Will"

Discernment lies at the heart of Christian spirituality. It is the art of appreciating the gifts that God has given us and discovering how we might best respond to them by putting them into use in daily living. It is a process of finding one's own way of being a disciple of Christ in a particular set of circumstances. It involves a response to the call of love and truth in a situation where choices often have to be made amidst conflicting interests and values. As a process, "discernment of spirits" is a gift by which we are able to observe and assess the different factors in a situation, and to choose that course of action that most authentically answers our desire to live by the gospel.[6]

Discernment is frequently associated with the difficult notion of "finding the will of God." Sometimes we talk about "the will of God" as though it were a large, living blueprint of what God wants to happen in the world. In this understanding, finding the will of God means locating that tiny area of the immense celestial blueprint that concerns us, and getting to know what God wants us to do so that we can comply and "do the will of God." This model, admittedly somewhat caricatured, is often the source of considerable anxiety to many good people who invest no small amount of time and energy in looking for "the will of God." They become very distressed when, not surprisingly, they do not succeed. Of the several reasons why this "management blueprint" model is unsatisfactory, the principal one is that it constricts our freedom so much. The range of our freedom is reduced to choosing to "fit in," whether we like it or not, with what God has "planned" for us—once we think we know what that is.[7]

A more satisfactory understanding of the will of God places a higher value on human freedom. In this approach, *God's will for us is that we should learn to respond in freedom to God's love for us, and to freely shape our lives by the choices that we make.* God has given us instruments to assist us in the responsible exercise of our freedom: conscience and powers of judgment, scripture, tradition, the church, friends, spiritual directors, and rules of discernment fashioned through careful testing over time, to name a few.[8]

What, then, can we say about "God's will"? David Lonsdale, involved for many years in adult Christian formation, provides this succinct summary:

> God's will is that we should exercise our freedom responsibly and well by choosing what honestly seems the best course of action in a given set of circumstances, using all the relevant aids that we have been given for that purpose. There is a sense in which we create, in terms of concrete action in given circumstances, the will of God in this exercise of freedom. There is no blueprint in God's mind with which we have to comply.[9]

When I was teaching English literature and coaching football and track in southern California in my mid-twenties, I said to myself: "There are a lot of people who would be very happy to be doing just what I'm doing, but for me helping kids appreciate good writing and how to throw a cross-body block or run hurdles is not enough. I want a more direct entrée to people's hearts. I want to talk with them about their deepest aspirations. I want to engage them in sharing our experiences of God and our struggle in faith to go deeper into that mysterious encounter." Shortly after, I joined the Paulists.

Each of us has a calling, a passion that burns inside us. It is so important that we access that secret place within ourselves and bring it forth into the light of day and begin living it until the energy flowing in our bodies sings its delight and confirms for us beyond the shadow of a doubt that we are onto our way, our path, our dharma work. We are where we are supposed to be, doing what the Creator of the universe is calling us to do.

The important thing for each of us is *that* we get on the rails of that work and roll—not *where* we do it. If we get in the dharma zone in one place and are called to a new place, we will just continue to do it there with new frameworks and formats. And because we are living out of our gifts and passion, it will free and empower others around us to do the same.

I have found the direct entrée to people's hearts that I was looking for in the leading of day-long, weekend, week-long retreats and ecumenical parish missions that bring together believers of different traditions. I have found a way to wed my twin passions for the spiritual life, on the one hand, and for Christian unity and interfaith understanding and respect on the other, by pursuing questions in the spiritual life in an ecumenical or interfaith context. In my twenty-six years of ecumenical ministry, the pastoral approach to what is called "spiritual ecumenism"—the coming together in prayer and the sharing of spiritual gifts among members of different traditions—has proven to be one of the best ways of preparing the members of our faith communities to actively welcome every new opportunity to express their unity in faith, life, worship, and service.

As each one of us seeks that particular art form that is our way of serving, it is not uncommon to find people operating out of the idea that God's will for us and our will for ourselves are at opposite ends of the spectrum. It is not impossible that such might be the case, but it is not likely for those who have committed their hearts and lives to God, who have committed to developing a personal relationship with God and living out the consequences of that relationship in their personal lives. When these conditions are present, there may be areas of our hearts that remain mission territory needing evangelization, but our deepest selves are united to God in an intimate relationship. When such is the case, pursuing that which is repugnant to us or allowing ourselves to be drained by what doesn't interest us is more likely a sin against the Holy Spirit. The degree to which we are exhausted is likely the degree to which we are working against the grain of God's gifts to us. These gifts are normally identified through our own deep yearnings; they do not work against them.

Still others view the will of God as rather like a ten-ton block of granite hanging overhead, ready to fall on them. Actually, the word that we translate into English as *will* comes from both a Hebrew and a Greek word that means "yearning." It is that yearning which lovers have for one another—not a yearning of the mind alone or of the heart alone but of the whole being.[10]

There is a wonderful story about a devout Jew who went to a holy man and said, "What is one thing I can do that will be seen as a good work in the sight of God?"

"How should I know?" he replied. "In your bible Abraham offered hospitality and God was with him. Elijah prayed and God was with him. David ruled his people and God was with him."

"But how shall I know what task God gives *me* to do?"

"Find the deepest inclination in your heart and follow it."[11]

We ask to know the will of God without guessing that it is written into our very beings. We perceive that will when we discern our gifts. Our obedience and surrender to God are in large part our obedience and surrender to our gifts. When we are clear about who we are and what we are doing, the energy flows freely. Desire generates power and physical energy. If we do not take desire for God and God's service seriously, we will have failed to utilize the greatest source of human vitality and passion that God has given us.[12] "Thy desire is thy prayer," said St. Augustine, "and if thy desire is without ceasing, thy prayer will be without ceasing....The continuance of your longing is the continuance of your prayer.[13]

As the poem that opened this chapter expressed it, "Ask not where the divine design for your life is written," for

It is written on your heart
in the colors of desire.
It is sung by the silent voices
of your recurring dreams.
It is the refrain chanted
by the chorus of your accumulating years:
"If not now, when? If not here, where?"
And the only obedience that will set you free is
                surrender
to the energy and fire congealed in your gifts.

The process of discerning our gifts and call is a process of surrender, not of control. The best way to let clarity come is to let it form on the roof of our consciousness and hit the page in droplets. Trusting this slow and random drip, we will be startled one day by the flash of "Oh! That's *it!*"[14] At the heart of it is invitation and response. As channels of God's own creative energies, we need to trust the darkness, to learn to let things percolate instead of boring straight ahead like a drill into a hard piece of wood.

The Self, as the subject of the unconscious, is always one step ahead of the ego, the subject of conscious experience, intellectual activity, and desire. That makes it impossible to *know* that what you are doing here and now is in line with the wisdom of the Self, since knowing is a function of consciousness. However, if one's will is steadfastly in the direction of the good and if one is willing to suffer when the good seems ambiguous, Self will always be one step ahead of the ego (*conscious* mind) in the right direction. The Holy Spirit will lead us and we will do the right thing—we just won't have the luxury of knowing it at the time![15]

Locating Our Deepest Desires

Even if we are in touch with our own inner world, it can be difficult to sort out and identify our innermost feelings and desires. And if we have been allowing our lives to be directed by the winds of external pressures, this sorting-out process will be even more difficult. The false self may have established itself with firm hands on the ship's rudder, allowing our boat to go in whatever direction the pleasing winds of praise and acceptance are blowing. The faint, whispering breeze from Self is drowned out by what the surrounding office, family, or societal culture wants or what other crew members say I should do. The false self's grip on the tiller must be wrested loose if our deepest inner yearnings at the level of the Self are to have a chance to fill our sails and direct our course. Without that, we will be manipulated by external gusts and stripped of the ability to steer our course according to the interior movements of the Holy Spirit.

Patrick is a consultant to high-tech companies. After losing his job, he struggled to get clear within himself what kind of work he really wanted to do, and to resist jumping at the first thing that came along. His description effectively illustrates how discernment involves keeping the false self and the messages it emits in the gallows so that ego can detect the breezes emanating from Self and align the sails accordingly.

We had been upbeat in our weekly review of sales prospects till a sickening pause in the phone conversation. In the remaining seconds, I was pushed off the company's edge down a slippery slope into the dark valley of No Income.

The sales team's desperation to close sales cut through the earlier commitments to sales professionalism, to customer focus and to long-term vision. Professional services are sold and purchased where there is a minimum foundation of mutual trust and respect. I had been building this trust with large potential clients over the preceding weeks and months. I had reviewed my approach, my plans and my progress, prospect by prospect, with the sales team. The feedback had been flattering: I was leading the way in applying global best practices in sales development to our company's business. Peers were asked to follow my lead. We knew the closing of major contracts would take many months and we were all committed to pressing forward with our adaptation of a proven approach.

The first sting was dishonesty. Why had no one said I was off-track? Too slow? Too ambitious? Or simply misguided? Or was it their lack of courage in confronting me when there was still time to get on track? Or if I was on track to deliver, why did no one signal that time was running out?

The second wave of stings were the terrors of self-doubt. Were the signals there all along but had I been too blind to see, too deaf to hear, or just too full of myself? With my customary enthusiasm and energy and task orientation, had I again (painful recollections of my wife's often too astute observations emerged from the pain-filled daze) simply not seen what was really going on in my team, in the company and with my customers?

Then the papers came. The company's own financial difficulties surfaced as a preposterous ploy to avoid paying me any severance. I was officially terminated for cause. The stings of humiliation and shame and powerlessness in the face of patent injustice. My indignation, outrage and fury were exceeded only by a nauseous panic.

We had never been able to put money aside. With four growing kids we had always only kept revenues just ahead of expenses. A financial planner years ago had unhelpfully advised us to change our lifestyle to allow for regular savings. Already we found our kids were so understanding in doing without so many goodies and gimmicks and consumables found at their friends, from single-child families or from those with divorced parents. We had always wanted to give more rather than to find ways to cut back even more.

No money in the bank. The new school year was beginning with all its expenses and demands. My professional self-confidence was shattered. My downward spiral emerged from the fusion of excessive self-reliance and undue attachment to the family's economic status quo. How would I pay the bills? How would I get the rest of the family to cut expenses right away? Turn off the lights when you leave your room! Take shorter showers! Eat less! Waste less!

Who would hire me? When? How would we survive till then? If only my resume would say this and not that! If only I were more technologically savvy! If only I had been, in my earlier career, less family focused and more interested in developing my business network! If only my wife had brought her own business network to our relationship! Why did I make so many mistakes in my career? Why do people not return my phone calls? Where are my friends now?

My desperation and panic were palpable. I was lost and out of control. I knew I could not let it show. But it did: in my edgy smile and driven tone of voice. I wanted to jump at anything that would bring a dollar to the door. I was gripped in a nightmare where my efforts alone were the foundation and prerequisite for any satisfactory outcome. I felt frighteningly alone (despite being surrounded by concerned and supportive immediate family and friends), professionally devastated (despite what many would consider a resume with many strengths and good marketability) and so, so afraid. For myself. For my family.

For myself? For my family? There was a huge disconnect between what I was living and what I prayed. Through all this, and going back almost a decade, I had been faithful to daily prayers, occasional fasts and weekly eucharist. Somewhere I had read: fear is essentially un-Christian. I had not really understood, but this provocative phrase had stuck and, in an unplanned moment of lucidity, it shook me to the core.

It did not happen suddenly. Nothing snapped. Rather unexpectedly yet slowly: like a lake freezing in a snow-flurried December, or like an obscure shoreline dawning on the unhurried horizon, the panic, the nausea, the desperation sublimated into a reawakened trust, a more humble yet more passionate readiness to listen to what witness God wished me to offer here and now in each breath, in each gesture and with each word from my lips. I rediscovered the peaceful excitement of confidant abandonment.

One prayer, more than others over the years, has captured both my desire to abandon myself to God's will and my utter inability to live in accordance with its words:

"O Holy Spirit, soul of my soul, I adore you. Enlighten me. Guide me. Strengthen me. Console me. Tell me what I must do. Let me hear your commands. I promise to try to do all that you desire of me, and to accept all that you permit to happen to me. Only let me know your will."

One hears a note of surrender in that prayer, echoing what Patrick describes as "confident abandonment." If our relationship with God is a relationship of love, it will involve some form of surrender. We relinquish control over our lives little by little as the relationship deepens. It is not an immature handing over of responsibility for ourselves and our lives to another, but a choice to actively collaborate with God. We increasingly place our confidence in the Holy Spirit to guide us. Discernment presupposes a context like this—a willingness to look at and appreciate the signs of God's love for us and, in response, a readiness to pay attention to the movements of the Spirit of God in our hearts and to follow where the Spirit leads.[16]

I have always read the parable of the talents (Matt 25:14–30)—in which God rewards the ones who took risks and doubled what they had been given but punishes the one who played it conservatively—to mean that God likes it when we "go for it"! When it comes time for us to choose between a cherished dream and a present occupation that no longer stimulates us, we might play it conservative and ignore the dream, blaming God for our discontent. We sometimes act like it's God's fault that we didn't adopt that child, change careers, move to a new place, or say "yes" to that invitation. We have tried to be sensible, rather than risking to see whether the universe would support some healthy extravagance. Julia Cameron observes that "one reason we are miserly with ourselves is scarcity thinking. We don't want our luck to run out. We don't want to overspend our spiritual abundance. Again, we are limiting our flow by anthropomorphizing God into a capricious parent figure."[17]

If we remember that God is a limitless source of energy and resources, we are more apt to tap our creative power effectively and confidently. When we change or make a decision, we find that the world around us expands to further and extend that decision. By reading the message of God written into our gifts and interests, we are directed to that path where we find friends, material resources, and meaningful work. Very often, opines Cameron, when we cannot seem to find an adequate supply, it is because we are insisting on a particular human source of supply.

Our desires should never be trivialized or disregarded. It is important, however, to step back from desires and pleasures to see where they lead. All feelings are just data for discernment. This means refraining from endorsing our initial reactions until their credentials have been checked out and validated.

7

Holistic Decision Making

If we are to live our calling fully, our choices and decisions must be free and unconflicted. To arrive at such wholehearted decisions, a sound method of discernment is needed. A method that has stood the test of time and is in increasing usage today is the one developed by Ignatius of Loyola in his Spiritual Exercises. The milieu in which he lived in sixteenth-century Spain was not unlike our own age in both its turmoil and its promise. One world was crumbling and another was painfully coming to birth. He was one of those whose religious genius guided the transition.

His genius lay in realizing that every human experience has a religious dimension and meaning for those who want to discover it. The discovery of the religious meaning of one's own inner experience is called the discernment of spirits. In his Spiritual Exercises, Ignatius codified the "Rules for the Discernment of Spirits," which he learned from his own personal experience. The cornerstone of Ignatian spirituality is that God can be found in all things. Nothing is insignificant, because at every moment the true Self and the false self are at work. Therefore, careful attention to one's inner desires is absolutely necessary if one wants to know God's desires for one's life.[1]

The particular genius of Ignatius was his explanation of the dynamics of three interrelated factors within the framework of a person's religious experience. The three factors are religious experience, reason, and affect. Ignatius provided a structure within which each of these finds a significant place. A coordination among them is established so that one comes to a truly holistic and integrated decision based on data coming from the mind, feelings, senses, bodily sensations, and the imagination.[2]

Integrating Reason, Affect, and Religious Experience

Ignatius describes three ways in which God can guide the person faced with choice. In the first way, God acts upon the individual in such a way that one experiences something deep within click into place, providing an intuitive sense of how one must proceed. Or one may experience such a total congruence between, on the one hand, what one feels one must do, and on the other, what one thinks God wants one to do, that the course of action is clear. It could also be a moment of peak religious experience in which one feels an inner sense of clarity and certainty about what to do. This personal "moment of truth" is not the fruit of long and careful reflection, but can spring suddenly upon the person without any previous identifiable cause. It comes like a forceful flash of insight that erases the need for a decision-making process. What is to be done is clear.[3]

The second way relates to one's emotions. Ignatius often speaks of "consolations" and "desolations." Our experiences in life produce both pleasant and unpleasant feelings within us. Either type can lead to God. For example, sorrow for one's sins is an *unpleasant* feeling, and joy in serving a loved one's needs is a *pleasant* feeling. Both orient a person to God. If one discerns that a feeling leads toward God, it is considered to be a consolation, even if it feels unpleasant. If it leads toward the false self and its desires, it is counted as a desolation. Desolations, too, can be accompanied by pleasant or unpleasant feelings. For example, in self-righteously judging another, I can experience a *pleasant* feeling of satisfaction with myself; failing for the hundredth time in an area of weakness produces the *unpleasant* feeling of despair. Both the pleasant feeling of smug self-satisfaction and the unpleasant feeling of despair represent a movement toward the false self and reliance upon its resources. They are both desolations.

Feelings are always data for discernment; they are not to be trusted in and of themselves until we discern where they are going. How does one know that the movement is toward God and not toward the false self? A movement is recognized by its fruits. Sometimes, however, it takes a long time before the fruits come clear. In that case, one looks carefully at the origin of the feeling and traces its progression to see where the movement is tending. Is it moving one closer to one's deep, authentic desire or away from it? The point is that one's feelings are important data, and one's authentic desire is an important touchstone in the discernment process.[4]

In the third way, the process of reasoning is highlighted. In one suggested exercise, picturing oneself on one's deathbed and recalling one's purpose for existing (for Ignatius: "to praise, reverence, and serve God"), the person is asked to list the pros and cons of various options in the situation requiring a decision, the advantages and disadvantages of each possible choice. In this exercise of the mind, one is asked to discern which decision one would sit most comfortably with in the face of death.[5]

The second and third ways, based on affectivity and reasoning, were designed by Ignatius to function in a complementary dynamic. The process seeks grounding in felt knowledge, not in theoretical abstractions. So in the process of discernment, one watches the continuity of thoughts *and* the feelings that float around these thoughts like clouds in the sky. The presumption is that the total organismic sensing of a situation is more trustworthy than the intellect alone or the feelings alone. It is a question of trusting the totality of one's experience which is, of course, still fallible, but more reliable than the conscious mind or feelings taken as the sole point of reference.[6]

Our technological, scientific western world mistrusts what it cannot quantify and empirically verify, but Christian tradition insists on including bodily reactions and intuitions amongst the data because it believes that no aspect of our lives escapes the influence of the Holy Spirit. Ignatius reminds us that God is in all things and can be encountered in our thought processes, our affective states, as well as in our religious experiences.[7]

Maria Teresa Porcile, a friend and biblical scholar who lived in Montevideo, Uruguay, died while this manuscript was in process. In her final months she lived an experience that exemplifies the way God can communicate with us through our bodily reactions and intuitions. At the beginning of the 1980s, we spent the better part of a year together at Bossey, the World Council of Churches' study center outside of Geneva, Switzerland. We became close friends and, thanks to the occasional international conference, remained in touch over the years. In 1999 she stayed at our residence while giving talks at the Canadian Theological Students Conference in Montreal.

In one of our first conversations, while we were bringing each other up to date on new engagements around which we felt some energy, I told her of the Facing Our Mortality retreat that

I had developed. She listened with keen interest and asked if I would share with her some of the meditations I used. For the next two weeks, she kept coming back to that, wanting to know more about the expression and focus of this retreat, the approach used, the rhythm of silence and word.

When she returned to Montevideo, she went in for her medical examination and an advanced stage of colon cancer was detected. The diagnosis led to an immediate surgical procedure. Soon, a postoperative complication developed, peritonitis, with a generalized infection throughout her body. They operated on her six times in the next eleven days, and she was close to death. Afterward, she wrote that she now realized that when I spoke to her about my retreat theme, "my body and soul were tuning into something that my purely rational awareness still had not grasped, namely, the fact of feeling, experiencing the approach of death halfway through life." Her body knew something that her mind had not yet become aware of: She would soon be facing her own mortality in dramatic terms.

What she shares of her experience in the various stages of convalescence further underlines how God can communicate with us through means other than words and concepts:

It is not easy to express this type of experience that many have had and which is a kind of passageway to another look at life. The experience of prayer when one is sick is something different; maybe the mystics would call it "passive." It is presence and memory of the heart; it is wordless, without concepts. At times everything boiled down to holding the rosary beads between my hands and caressing them. But finally it all came down to repetition of the Name (of

Jesus). Friends became the vehicle of God's love; they became sacraments enfleshed.

I was living a kind of rain shower of affection, strings or chains of love and prayer that were pure gifts of grace. I felt various types of presence. This presence has accompanied me in this whole process: the presence of men and women friends, the presence of the saints on earth and in heaven, the presence of God. This presence came in the form of greetings, cards, flowers. For a person going through this "health adventure," the theme of the presence of others, which becomes a sacramental presence of immense love, is fundamental.

I kept feeling that at every level it is true: *only love saves.* Including love that becomes science, study, hard work, exhaustion, attentiveness, care and wisdom on the part of the doctors and nurses and all the people accompanying me. Each presence, in whatever form it took, became a kind of stitch in the fabric which sheltered life.

In the midst of these situations there is a strange peace, close to happiness, with the flavor of a beatitude. "Blessed are the meek, for they shall inherit the earth." So often "nothing changes," but eyes and heart can change (as happened to Job). We are all familiar with hospital or hospice rooms which become in some instances, by living "wounded love," spacious places where silence speaks, sings, and announces the presence of God. This is a paradoxical and non-transferable happiness, secret, intimate — the happiness of vulnerability which becomes pure receptivity to Love. It is the secret of the Gospel, the most profound aspect of being human.

A human-sacramental dimension is given to the Body of Christ. I know that my experience of intensive care was like an experience of the body-as-eucharist, lived in my own body. I felt that my body was open, exposed, poured out. Little by little, my view of the body became love poured out....

I felt death, I felt it with peace, and at the same time it didn't seem to me to be time. I began to think about living, and saw myself giving courses, taking part in congresses, writing. I thought of my commitments, plans and projects for the year ahead. And I realized that all of this was not sufficient motive for me to live.

Then, unexpectedly, I was reminded of something, the memory of something real: a meeting I had with a little five-year-old girl from a school that I visited on behalf of a special program in Latin America. This girl had pursued me into the recreation yard of her school, asking me, "Are you coming tomorrow?" To my surprise this little girl "visited me" in intensive care, and in her the whole world was compressed, concentrated: the girl, the world, was asking for my attention, love, protection, gentleness, and caress. I became aware that her particular face was more fundamental for me than all that was purely conceptual; it meant more than all the professional research, no matter how stimulating it might be.

She did not consciously know when she was with me in Montreal that she was not well, but her body knew and was giving her subtle signals that only became intelligible later in hindsight. And how could she ever have known that it would be the little five-year-old girl who had followed her into the school yard who would help her at the crossroad between death and life to choose to continue her struggle to live by asking her: "Are you coming tomorrow?" Truly, God can use everything to direct our steps! Feelings, bodily sensations, memories, chance encounters, as well as thoughts. This is why Ignatius's method of discernment takes into account intuition, different affective movements of consolation and desolation, and all the reasons for and against the various options. Everything is data for discernment: "Test everything; hold fast to what is good" (1 Thess 5:21).

Choose Life

When my sister graduated from college, the program cover for the ceremony carried the following words by Helen Kelley: "Choose life—only that and always and at whatever risk. Christ came that we might have life and have it more abundantly. The world is full of false prophets who will tell you otherwise. To let life leak out, to let it wear away by the mere passage of time, to withhold giving it and spending it, is to choose nothing. The ultimate betrayal of your faith and your education is not to choose life with all of the anguish and terror and delight which are attendant upon that choice."

I was inspired by those words then, and still am now. They communicate to me a clear sense that God's dream for the world is like an immense mosaic, and everyone has his or her piece of glass to contribute to it. We are allowed to choose the color and even where to place our piece. And if we don't, there will be empty spaces in the mosaic. There is an overarching action of

God in the world that serves as the touchstone for each one's use of gifts and talents in response to God's call.

In Ignatius's vision, human beings are created for community with the Triune God and thus with one another. All the other things on the face of the earth are created to help us to attain to this experience of communion and community. The whole universe is shot through with that one intention.

In the view of theologian Walter Brueggemann, the central vision of world history in the Bible is that all creation is one, every creature in community with every other, living in harmony and security toward the joy and well-being of every other creature. "The most staggering expression of the vision," he writes, "is that *all persons are children of a single family*, members of a single tribe, heirs of a single hope, and bearers of a single destiny...."[8] God is always working to bring about community and harmony between people and the whole created universe. We can be completely in tune with that intention, partially in tune with it, or totally out of tune with it. Our aim in living our vocation fully is to become attuned to God's one action and intention, to *become* people who do in fact find God in all things, even in the midst of the demands of family life and professional careers.[9]

One of the truly remarkable human beings of the twentieth century, Václav Havel, demonstrates for all of us what a difference one person's dedicated service can make. He led the "velvet revolution" in Czechoslovakia in 1989 in which, without a shot being fired, the Czech communist government (in the face of thousands of people holding vigil in the streets), resigned, and free elections were held. Havel was subsequently first elected president of the new democratic government of Czechoslovakia, and then of the Czech Republic. In his book *Living in Truth* he shares the fundamental conviction that motivated him during eight years of imprisonment:

> All of us, East and West, face one fundamental task from which all else should follow. That task is one of resisting vigilantly, thoughtfully and attentively, but at the same time with total dedication, at every step and everywhere, the irrational momentum of anonymous, impersonal and inhuman power....We must not be ashamed that we are capable of love, friendship, solidarity, sympathy, tolerance, but just the opposite: we must set these fundamental dimensions of our humanity free from their "private" exile and accept them as the only genuine starting point of meaningful human community.[10]

When we are not ashamed that we are capable of love, sympathy, and solidarity, the communion with God that defines the deep nature of each person then moves from being an unconscious mystery to being a conscious reality that shapes every choice and action. When we are in tune with the one action of God in our own actions, we become active agents for the reign of God in the world. Our vocation is not simply to *be*, but to work together with God in creation, to work with God in creating our own identity and the particular way in which we will contribute to becoming who we are as sons and daughters of God. The seeds that God has planted in my Self are the seeds of my own identity, my own reality, my own happiness. To use my freedom to refuse them is to refuse my identify, my Self. Not to freely choose to actively and consciously collaborate with God's intention for the world is to refuse the fullness of my existence. As Albert Schweitzer said, "I don't know what your destiny will be, but one thing I know: the only ones among you who will be really happy are those who have sought and found how to serve."[11]

God desires that each of us be in tune with God's one action in our actions. When we are not in tune, we experience ourselves as alienated, unhappy, unfulfilled, even though we cannot identify the source of the malaise. On the other hand, we have probably all had experiences of being "in the flow," of firing on all cylinders, of being right where we are meant to be, doing exactly what we are meant to be doing. William A. Barry describes the experience:

> If you have ever experienced a time when you were "in the flow," able to live with relative unambivalence and lack of fear in the now, attuned to the presence of God, then you have an idea of what it might be like to be at one with the one action of God. In such a state you are a contemplative in action. You know that you are at the right place at the right time. There are no doubts about whether you should be someone else or somewhere else. You do not need to justify being married or single or a religious; it is right to be who you are here and now. And you live and act comfortably with the knowledge of your own limitations, of your finitude, of your small part in the immense history of the world. To be attuned to the one action of God, to his will, is to be extraordinarily free, happy and fulfilled even in the midst of a world of sorrow and pain.[12]

8

An Experience of Call

To recapitulate our reflection on this theme, I will use an experience of call that emerged in my life. My purpose is not to dwell on the events of my life as such, but to lay down that life experience and reflect on it as a kind of case study with an eye toward how it reflects the themes in this chapter. My narrative is but a takeoff point for your own reflection on how the experience of call in your life manifested itself, how you discerned your response to it, and where you find support and strength in faithfully adhering to it.

In 1991, following the World Council of Churches General Assembly in Canberra, Australia, I went on a three-month sabbatical to India. I had been working for ten years at the Canadian Center for Ecumenism in Montreal, Quebec. The center had both ecumenical and interfaith departments. My particular area of involvement was on the ecumenical side: the work for increasingly visible unity among the various denominational Christian churches through worship and common life, witness and service to the world. After ten years of serving on national dialogues, organizing summer institutes, preaching ecumenical parish missions, and leading educational seminars for Christian clergy and laity, I wanted to get a better sense of the dynamics in interfaith dialogue and collaboration. So I elected to go to India: It was proximate to Australia, and one could enter into an experience there with Hindus, Buddhists, and Muslims in their home context (there are more Muslims in India than in any other country of the world save Indonesia).

On my way to India, I reflected in my journal how I had intended to spend about ten years at the Center for Ecumenism, and observed that I was at the ten-year mark. "God," I said, "I am going to try to be a *tabula rasa* during this sabbatical time. If you have any desires for me, please make them known." My first place of study was in South India, Shantivanam Ashram, where Father Bede Griffiths tutored me in a reading of the Upanishads and the Bhagavad Gita.

When I left Shantivanam, I went to Tiruvannamalai and stayed at the ashram of Sri Ramana Maharshi, a Hindu mystic of the twentieth century who had a riveting experience of his Self as a young man, and around whom an ashram (a place where those wishing to deepen their spiritual lives go) grew up and continues to this day, even though he has been dead since 1950. From there my itinerary took me to Pondichery on the coast of the Indian Ocean, where sits the ashram of Sri Aurobindo, another twentieth-century Hindu divine whose teaching holds great resonance with that of the Jesuit mystic and paleontologist Teilhard de Chardin. Then I set my compass due north toward the Divine Life Society's Shivananda Ashram in Rishikesh, a town noted for its concentration of "rishis" or sages, where the headwaters of the Ganges run clear and cold out of the foothills of the Himalayas.

In each one of these places, I met what to my mind was an inordinate number of Westerners. Our conversations invariably turned to why we had come. The things people said began to fall into a pattern and became distressingly familiar: "Christianity doesn't teach us practical methods and means to enable us to go deeper in the spiritual life. So we have come here looking for someone who will teach us things we need to know." The more I heard comments of this nature, the more I began to reflect on what I knew of church life in the Western world and to examine it critically in the light of what these people were saying. An exchange on the subject with a local swami only intensified the exercise. When asked why so many people were leaving Western religions for those of the East, the swami responded, "Because Judaism and Christianity are not teaching them practically. I am teaching them practically. Love of God is being taught both in the Bible and the Bhagavad Gita. But today's religionists are not actually teaching *how* to love God. I am teaching how. That is the difference."

In the larger picture, all the experiences I was having were only confirming me in the ecumenical and interfaith work that I was doing. I continued to invite God to give me any new signals that God might have for me, but what was coming through in my experiences was: "You're right where I want you. When I have something new for you, you'll know it. In the meantime, just relax with the question." At my next stop, the Tushita Buddhist Retreat Center at Dharamsala, the Dalai Lama's colony in the Himalayas, something happened.

I was participating in a ten-day intensive course called "The Graduated Path" in Buddhist doctrine and meditation methods (again, with a group made up *entirely* of Westerners). While sitting quietly one afternoon in meditation, something that I can only describe as a "message" flashed across the screen of my consciousness like a shooting star and landed with a thud. When I opened my eyes at the end of the period and returned to my room, it was with a clear sense that when I got home I was to become involved in the founding of a center for spirituality where the many pathways by which people could come to God would be competently addressed and reliable accompaniment provided. When the retreat ended, I came down from the Himalayas to the Henry Martyn Center for Islamic Studies in Hyderabad in central India to participate in an intensive course on Islam.

When I arrived back in the United States in June to visit family, one of the first things I did was to telephone one of my friends in the Paulists to tell him about the inner movement of the spirit that had occurred for me in India. The "message" remained sharp and active within me. I spent an additional month working on drafts of two books that flowed directly out of my experience in India. I wanted to make my own contribution to redress the oft-heard critique of Christianity not getting down to the "how" of loving God. Both books dealt with concrete and practical ways of deepening one's spiritual life and relationship with God.[1]

Surprises Back Home

Toward the end of the summer, I reported on the sabbatical experience in general and the inspiration for an ecumenical center for spirituality in particular to one of the members of the Paulist presidential board. I returned to Montreal in August and soon became immersed in the work at the Canadian Center for Ecumenism. In the fall I was invited to participate in a think-tank group that was engaged in creative visioning for a prime property that had been vacated while I was away by the Benedictines of Montreal and given to the archdiocese.

In the 1980s, the house had become a mecca for people being caught up in the renewal of contemplative prayer, or Christian meditation, as John Main called it. Dom John Main, the original prior of the house, was one of the principal catalyzers of a renewal movement of Christian contemplative prayer, beginning with the meditation center he opened at Ealing Abbey in England in 1974 before coming to Montreal in 1977. After Main's death in 1982, the Benedictines continued for another nine years before turning the house over to the archdiocese and disbanding to other places. A dedicated group of laypeople, many of whom had become Benedictine associates or oblates, kept the Monday and Tuesday evening meditation groups going and organized a monthly prayer day. But apart from that, the house was not being used.

When our group met in November to brainstorm new uses for the house, it did not even occur to me to think of it in the light of the inspiration I had received in India. My thoughts in that regard were focused on the Paulist novitiate property twenty-seven miles outside of New York City, set on a sloping hill leading to a small lake and surrounded by twelve hundred acres of wooded land. The think-tank group did not come up with any ideas that generated enthusiasm in every corner. We agreed to engage our creative thought processes and to meet again in the new year.

Testing the Spirits

Within the following month, while I was meditating one morning, the thought bubbled up: Was I supposed to make a connection between what I had received in India and the availability of this property? After meditation, I came back to that thought and decided that there was only one way to find out: Put the idea out there and see how the group responded. The group leaders liked the idea and encouraged me to take it directly to the chancellor of the archdiocese who was acting as president of the board that had been set up to oversee the house and property.

So I did. He, too, reacted favorably, saying he knew of a charitable foundation that might respond positively to the ecumenical nature of the project and might be inclined to contribute to it financially. He asked me to put it in writing and present it to the other members of the board at their next meeting.

I drew up a three-phased plan and presented it to them. Their response, too, was positive. They directed me to present it to the cardinal archbishop. I began to get clammy. Things were spiraling upward quickly. If he liked the idea, something could really happen. Was I *ready* for something to happen?

I finally got in to see Cardinal Turcotte in July. Following the meeting, I wrote in my journal:

July 6, 1992: I went in to talk to Archbishop Turcotte today. We talked for two hours, and the item which generated the most energy and held us the longest was my proposal for an ecumenical Center for Christian Spirituality. He has been praying over how best to use the house and property, too, and had asked four religious communities to join their prayers to his own. Our visions resonated strongly with one another on all the essential points: a place where people learn how to pray; ecumenical participation; residential community of ecumenical composition; women and men;

French and English. He said that several proposals for use of the house had come before him, but he had said, "No, not that. Not that. Nor that." "This is the first thing I am hearing," he said, "that makes my heart leap up." Before we finished, he raised the leadership question. "In listening to you, I recognize someone in whom I would have confidence. I know your ecumenical experience. I know your empathy with people. I know your commitment to prayer. And in your years here, you have adapted well to the francophone milieu. Would you be willing to give five years to help us get this up and going?"

I told him that I wasn't looking for a new job, that there was no one waiting in the wings to step in for me and direct the Center for Ecumenism, but that if this was where the Spirit was calling, I hoped I could be open to hear it and respond. He said he had heard enough for the time being, and wanted to consult next with the leaders of the other churches in the city to see if it they would be interested in such a project.

We both left on summer holidays. From my place on an island in the middle of Lake George, New York, I made the following inscription in my journal:

For the past few years I've felt the Spirit preparing me for a next evolutionary step. My growing interest in spirituality and the increased number of unsolicited invitations I've received to do work in that area have been signals to me that this way lies my future. My taste for sharing with people interested in the spiritual life and in an experience of loving intimacy with God has become so pronounced that I feel sure the Spirit is leading me into this. The way everyone to whom I have presented the idea for a Center for Spirituality has positively responded is yet more confirmation.

I must not cling to my present security (e.g., the good staff at the ecumenical center with whom I enjoy working, our relative financial security) nor react with aversion to the prospect of sacrifice and suffering (e.g., moving from intimate living space where I have my own life with two people whose company I enjoy to a large place with more people where private space and a personal life will be harder to come by). Lord, help me to cling to nothing, void myself of all attachments, and keep myself free and open to respond to where the greater good seems to lie.

Consulting with Others

A member of a society of apostolic life doesn't make decisions on his or her own. One generally joins a community to work with others in its particular area of mission focus. Deployment of personnel is made through an open process of consultation and dialogue. I had earlier written to the president of the community appraising him of the evolving possibilities for my ministry in Montreal. I now wrote to him again putting the question the archbishop had put to me and asking if the community would be interested in supporting this new endeavor through my participation in it. The response was cautious: Go forward slowly, keep us abreast of new developments. One of the Paulist mission domains is ecumenical and interfaith work; there was a responsible reticence around my leaving the directorship of an established national ecumenical and interfaith center for something not yet existing that might not ever get off the ground.

In February of 1993, the leaders of the major churches in the city, and those delegated with responsibility for interim activities in the former Benedictine Priory met at the house. They were unanimous in their positive response to the idea and its potential, and demonstrated a readiness to immediately move toward action. When I raised the question of finances, the Roman Catholic chancellor responded: "Don't worry about the money now. Just begin. If this is of the Holy Spirit, the money will come."

By April, each of seven participating denominations had named a representative to an interchurch planning committee charged with responsibility for getting the wheels under a year-long pilot project to test the viability of the venture. The committee worked steadily on a mission statement, programming, and staff needs. A temporary house manager came forward and offered his services, and by midsummer we delivered program brochures to the various church offices for distribution within their networks. Shortly after that, I made a notation in my journal:

September 13, 1993: The Center for Spirituality opened two days ago. I received some inspiration in India in April-May 1991 and came back with a dream but no clear idea of what to do with it. Twenty-four months after my return, the brochure for it is out and it has opened its doors. Lord, you do wondrous things!

I told my spiritual director that in the year ahead I wanted to focus on the question of where the Lord was calling me in relation to my work at the Canadian Center for Ecumenism and the evolution taking place at the new ecumenical Center for Spirituality and Christian Meditation. In our November meeting, he said, "The light you seek will probably come as a result of searching for solutions. For every step forward you're able to mark, there may be two or three missteps. But over time and with repeated efforts, things become clearer."

Word had come in from my Paulist superior, with whom I had been in periodic communication, that the new project looked promising, and that I was being given the green light if I wanted to "go for it." Shortly thereafter, aware that the time of decision making was being pushed to a new level for me personally, I decided to make my annual week-long retreat in the house. I had never spent more than an overnight in it and had certainly never felt drawn to live in it. I was prepared to see others inhabit it but didn't see myself among them. I was curious to see what it felt like to spend several days in the place. My spiritual director's counsel to me as we talked about the upcoming retreat was to ask for a particular grace and to keep an open, empty space within for listening.

Personal Retreat: A Turning Point

As I began the retreat on April 4, 1994, the grace I asked for was this: "Lord, to trust you unreservedly to let me know what you want of me, and in that trust, to know peace." My workbook for the retreat was *Discovering Your Gifts, Vision, and Call.*[2]

Each day I worked through the questions posed in the exercises at the end of each chapter: What are my unique gifts? How can I call forth another's gifts? Which vision is mine to carry? What is God calling me to do? How can I work together with those who share my call? How can the larger community share the callings of its members?

Over the next few days I tried to just let the thoughts, feelings, and fantasies arise without editing them, just observing them. The fantasies were all in the direction of being there—*living* there—and seeing different things happen. Seeing the dream-inspiration that came to me in India of an ecumenical center for spirituality where people could come and learn the practical disciplines for the Christian life. Seeing a vibrant contemplative community made up of women and men, laity and clergy, at the heart of the city. All the feelings coming up were positive. I felt the pieces coming together and falling into place. To my amazement, in the face of all my reservations about living there, fantasies were coming up of moving out of my present residence at the end of the summer. The words of Goethe kept coming into my mind. They were, in fact, words that never seemed to leave me.

Until one is committed, there is hesitancy, the chance to draw back, always ineffectiveness concerning all acts of initiative and creation. There is one elementary truth the ignorance of which kills countless ideas and splendid plans: that the moment one definitely commits oneself, then Providence moves, too. All sorts of things occur to help one which would otherwise never have occurred. A whole stream of events issues from the decision, raising in one's favor all manner of unforeseen incidents and meetings and material assistance which no man could have dreamed would come his way. Whatever you can do, or dream you can, begin it. Boldness has genius, power, and magic in it. Begin it now.

In the gospel reading for the final day of my retreat, Jesus appeared to his disciples and said, "Peace be with you. Why are you frightened and why do doubts arise in your hearts?...It is I myself" (Luke 24:38). I reflected on the week past in my journal:

April 9: The grace I asked for has been granted: I have come to a sense of where I can best use the gifts God has given me to serve. And I am at peace with it.

I am amazed at how quickly things turned inside. From April 4 to April 8, something rolled over, something opened, something went "click." For at least three years I have felt the Holy Spirit preparing me for some new step that would be in continuity with my past and would yet be *new*.

The week's retreat here has been like that bend in the road where, on my first trip to Europe, after having read about Mount Blanc as the highest of the Alps and journeying toward it for days, all of a sudden it was looming up in front of me—huge, beautiful, beckoning. That's how this vision of the future feels. And I feel excitement within, eagerness to finally get out of the car and start hiking.

Trusting in the guidance, the peace, the inner clarity that has come to me in a steady stream through this week of silent listening, I am ready to move in over the summer and to give myself to the work that lies before us here.

In my next meeting with my spiritual director, I recounted the experiences of the retreat. He affirmed the process and the decision, recognizing that it came from within me. Meanwhile, other parallel processes were at work, causing things to unfold quickly. The interchurch steering committee that had been overseeing the operation in its first year had judged the experimental pilot phase a success. The project was clearly responding to a need; the desire now was to plan for the future and put it on a firmer footing. Toward that end, a selection committee had been formed to hire a Director. About three weeks after my retreat, a phone call came from the head of the committee calling me to a leadership role at the new Center. That night, I sat quietly in my room and wrote in my journal:

> So there it is. In the end, it comes quietly, without fanfare, just with an inner sense of my own discernment process being confirmed by the discernment of the selection committee. After the phone call, I got up and stood in front of my icon of Christ the Pantocrator and made a deep bow to the One who was holding open the Book of Life on which the following words appear: "You have not chosen me, but I have chosen you to go forth and bear fruit."

Summary

To clearly situate this personal account as a case study in the theme of this chapter—holistic decision making—it may be helpful to summarize the three ways Ignatius describes in which God can guide a person faced with a decision.

In the first way, God acts upon the individual in such a way that one experiences something deep click into place, providing an intuitive sense of how one must proceed. It can spring suddenly upon one without any previous identifiable cause. What is to be done is clear.

The second way relates to one's emotions. Feelings, whether pleasant or unpleasant, are always data for discernment. One looks carefully at the origin of the feeling and traces its progression to see where the movement is tending. Is it moving one closer to one's deep, authentic desire or away from it?

In the third way, the process of reasoning is highlighted. "What do you *really* want? Where lies the greater good?"

If one were to use my own story as a kind of case-study application of these three ways, one could see my experience while meditating at the Tushita Buddhist retreat center as an exemplification of the first way. I had been asking God to let me know if God had anything new in mind for me. One day, while simply sitting open and relaxed in meditation, there was an illuminating experience. I got up from the experience, went to my room, and began journaling about starting an ecumenical center for spirituality and describing in detail what it might look like. Although I did not know how or where or with whom this would come about, there was ever after within me a sense that it *would* come about if I opened myself to it responsively. What needs to be noted here as well is that the after-effects of such an experience must be scrutinized. Ideas and plans that are given in the time after an inspiration are not necessarily given by God and need to be tested.

The interest, energy, excitement, and stimulation I felt around this "call" could be taken as illustrative of the second way. These were feelings that remained constant throughout. The third way finds expression in my reflective process in journaling; testing the idea with the leaders of the brainstorming group and then the officials of the archdiocese; when it appeared that something could come of it, contacting my Paulist superiors to get their input; talking it through with a spiritual director whose task is to help the directee to know what he or she authentically desires.

The process of prayerfully sifting through all the data and looking at the religious experience, cognitive reflections, and affective states took place in my week's retreat at the house. It wasn't until then that I felt free and unconflicted enough to make a wholehearted decision and to step across the line of no return and really give myself to the project, come what may.

I think that many people have a touchstone experience of God. We need to pay more attention to those moments when we feel our hearts burning within us. Sometimes it is only in talking about such experiences with others that we recognize, after the fact and in the telling, how important they are to us.[3]

The call, in one form or another, is generally to step out into the deep, to choose life, and to live it to the full. It is the road to spiritual freedom.

Reflection Questions

A. When you are seeking to discern the movement of God's Spirit in your life, what do you look for? What kind of a process do you follow?

B. How have you tended to think about God's will in your life,

—as a kind of living blueprint of what God wants for you, something that you need to discover so that you can follow it?

—as an invitation to learn to respond in freedom to God's love for you, freely shaping your life by the choices that you make; something you co-create?

C. Can you identify a deep yearning that has remained constant in your life like an underground stream? How are you responding to that yearning now?

D. Was there ever a time in your life when you allowed yourself to be drained by something that didn't interest you?

Step Three

Let Go of Results

Letting Go

The hardest thing in living
is to receive a grace
a child, a friendship, a fulfilling work
and rejoice in it for the time
it is given
without clinging
without trying to prolong
its visitation.
The pull is so strong
to close around the feeling
the security offered
the identity given
the comfort found;
to lock it up
and possess it

to freeze the flow
of time and events
saying "Here. Now. Forever!"
But frozen goods
break the teeth.
Better to embrace
the thawed, life-giving moment
in open hearted thanks
carrying the gift lightly
in one's hands without grasping,
receiving it as promise and call
to live on the edge of divine desire,
allowing the inner urgent longing
to daily make the blood run
and keep the eyes open and focused,
squinting in the sun towards
the horizon of our Ultimate Hope.

9
A Personal Story

We named the new ecumenical center for spirituality and Christian meditation "Unitas," Latin for "unity." There was a vocation in the name: unity among the various participant churches; unity in the marriage of an ecumenical center for spirituality with the former Christian meditation center; unity among English speakers and French speakers; and unity of the whole person in the spirituality we wanted to foster. It was a name indicating God's own predilection, so evident in the world of flora and fauna: diversity in unity. A press conference was held at the house to which seven journalists came. Unitas was in the news.

The formal opening in September of 1994 exceeded all our expectations. There wasn't even standing room only in the chapel for the people who came; they were backed up into the corridor outside for the opening ecumenical service of prayer. The various church leaders were in attendance, and the Orthodox representative went through the house following the service, blessing each room according to their custom. A reception followed. When all the guests had gone, I went into the chapel and laid down on the floor on my back (this was not a chapel with pews or even chairs, but meditation cushions), staring at the ceiling, thinking: After all the discernment, discussion, prayer, reflection, it's actually happening! Our first guest, in what I took as a "wink" from God, was a journalist from India who was interested in writing us up.

The honeymoon, as they say, was short-lived. We were in a big, beautiful mansion, but with next to no money for salaries. So we dealt with the currency we did have—living space—and offered people room and board in return for their assistance in running the house.

Complex beings that we are, I was at the same time within myself celebrating this new beginning and mourning the letting go of my work situation at the Canadian Center for Ecumenism: the enjoyment of working with a team of professional colleagues, the convenience of the center's wonderful research library, the efficiency made possible by all the coordinated technology of computers, fax, and photocopy machines, the security of the endowment fund behind the operation. The prospect of starting from scratch at Unitas to build a team, raise money, beg secondhand equipment was staring me in the face, and part of me mourned the crazy company of my colleagues at the Ecumenical Center, where one could get a lot done in a short time because of their respective competencies and still have fun doing it. But the sense of call I felt to give myself to this new undertaking remained constant and clear, like a subterranean stream.

It was clearly going to be all uphill, however. We were receiving help from a foundation, but needed another $100,000 to cover staff salaries and program and publicity expenses. Revenues were coming in from guests, retreat and program fees, but not enough; we were looking at a $45,000 shortfall. Money was slow coming from the churches. The scenario stripped me of any hope I had of being able to move things forward by hiring a few professional staff at decent salaries for areas like the kitchen and office. We were going to have to find another way.

"You have to begin like that," a friend wrote me soon after. "That is the kind of scenario which, like St. Paul's 'glorying in his own weakness,' makes you rely totally on the help of God— makes you realize completely the truth that is always there but which we generally forget: Without God, we can do nothing. This is the way of the gospel: poor, simple, service-oriented, relying on God for everything."

I was looking for security, for control, for predictability—and there was none. In my journal I wrote:

> Why don't I just throw caution, security, and control to the winds and just give myself to it like a fool for Christ? Why don't I just do it as an experiment in faith? Why don't I just give myself to it and see what it has to teach me? Why don't I come across with an uncharacteristically wild act of abandon! Why don't I enter into an adventure of living with the real freedom of spirit that marks those who truly rely on God as their sufficiency? Why don't I just "go for it" and leave plenty of room for the God of surprises?

Well, we "went" for it, but it didn't look very glamorous in the day-to-day reality. We cobbled together a working staff, and over the course of the next year and a half met the crises that arose with growing confidence in our own process as a group and in our resiliency as individuals. Living in the mixed residential community of six felt normal and healthy.

By 1996 (fifteen months later), on every front, there were signs of progress. A board of directors was in place, working on bylaws and incorporation. The financial picture, too, was looking very healthy. The previous year, movie companies had discovered that we were open to renting space to them for location shoots. It was disrupting and invasive, but it also was the windfall we needed to continue. We learned to do our programmatic dance around their wires and cameras and cables, using floors that they were not occupying. How many people have the opportunity to get up from the supper table, walk into the next room, and watch Nick Nolte, Ben Kingsley, Megan Follows, Donald Sutherland, Aidan Quinn, Jennifer Love Hewitt, or George Hamilton shoot a scene? The revenues we realized from renting space in the house to film companies for about six weeks a year enabled us to run a retreat center and do what we wanted to do in the house the other forty-six weeks. It had its inconveniences, especially for the residents, but overall it was a win-win situation. All in all, we were coming into cruising speed and beginning to see the fruits of our labors.

Then came a call from my community to leave Montreal and open a new Paulist North American office for ecumenical and interfaith relations in New York City. At the Paulist community's 1994 General Assembly (the highest decision-making assembly of members, held every four years), the delegates had passed a resolution to give clearer witness to our commitment to Christian unity and interfaith understanding by opening a center or an office to guide our efforts. It was the responsibility of the president of the community to see that these resolutions had effective follow-up.

In the summer of 1997 he came to talk with me about it. Practically my whole ministry had been spent in ecumenical work, and when he looked around the community for someone to undertake this project on the community's behalf, my experience moved me to the top of his list of candidates. I went into the encounter praying to be like bamboo—empty, able to bend in the wind: not clinging to Unitas, not clinging to Montreal, not clinging to Canada. Just clinging to my desire to do what the Lord asks, to go where the Spirit directs, and praying for the grace of inner freedom. Free to stay, free to go. I was in search of passionate detachment.

The meeting was inconclusive; he could see that I was fully engaged where I was, and said that nothing would happen until our next General Assembly a year hence. Over the next several months, the theme of passionate detachment unfolded in my journaling:

November 7, 1997: Let it come, Lord; whatever you want. Just give me the inward assurance that it *is* what you want—whether staying to oversee the development of Unitas or going to begin something new. Keep me mindful that I am a member of a *missionary* society. Missionaries plant and move on. They don't cling to what they've begun, but give it over to others to take to the next stage of development. Grant me the grace of inner freedom. Freedom to stay and be grateful; freedom to move on to something new and be happy. Put the false self in irons and let me know the wonderful inner freedom that comes when one is but a tin whistle pressed to your lips.

On the first day of the new year, I put a picture of the angel Gabriel appearing to Mary in the annunciation in a place in my room where it would meet my eyes several times a day. I knew that to make her response to Gabriel my own would be my biggest challenge in the year ahead: "I am the servant of the Lord. Be it done unto me according to your word."

In the summer of 1998, the Paulist General Assembly met again. It not only reiterated the resolution of the previous assembly to create an office for ecumenical and interfaith relations for the community, but this time established a time line by which it wanted to see it happen. At the end of July I received a phone call from our president asking me to take on that challenge. He said he would give a year's advance notice to the board and staff and that a letter to that effect would be sent to them as well as to the church leaders.

Our whole staff team went away on retreat together for two days in September to digest the news and to look at the year ahead together. We went to the Paulist summer house on the shores of Lake George, New York. I think it was helpful for them to see over 140 years of pictures on the walls of men who have served the community's mission. It provided a tangible context in which they could see me as a member of a community and understand better the community's call upon me.

"The best homage we can give you," said one "is that you *can* leave. A good foundation has been laid, and a style has evolved which does not all depend on you." And from another came these words, which I felt were particularly insightful: "I see a maturation of your relationship with your community in this. You are receiving a call from your community, and you are deciding to honor it. In its own way, this affirmation can be as important as the work you are doing at Unitas."

As we got into the work of the fall season of programs and retreats, I dialogued with my journal:

I'm feeling good about what is unfolding. There will surely be things I miss—friends, mixed community, speaking French, Mount Royal, schedule built around meditation, my room, the garden, this lovely, walkable city. The whole living situation has been both gift and privilege, and will provide me with ample opportunity to demonstrate that I can enjoy the gifts given without clinging to them, to carry them lightly and let them go for another's enjoyment when the time comes. There is some dying ahead, but there is also the promise of new life!

I had no idea of the "dying" that lay ahead.

In January 1999, the church leaders had scheduled a lunch and meeting at Unitas. My phone conversation with one of the bishops reassured me that it was basically an opportunity for them to check in with one another in our leadership transition year, to see whether everybody was still on board, and to share with one another their own thoughts about the kind of person who should be looked for as my successor. For my part, we had a good report to make. Unitas had been financially in the black five years running—not something to be taken for granted in retreat centers. One of our residents, a sociologist by training, had just completed a study of patterns of participation in our programming. For the first time, we had an idea of just how many people were coming, from where, and for what. The numbers surprised even us. In the past year, there had been approximately 9,500 participants in our events.

The meeting was all I had understood it would be, and more. *Much* more. It took an unexpected turn in light of some projected building maintenance costs that were in excess of what any of the churches wanted to be responsible for. By the time the meeting ended, the church leaders had reached a consensus that the house should be sold. They reiterated their support and enthusiasm for the work that we were doing, but expressed the conviction that a more affordable place in which to do it could be found. They sent a recommendation to the Unitas board to find a new location as soon as possible.

When I had seen the last church leader out the door, I went into the chapel and sat down. I was stunned, in a state of semi-shock. I remembered the afternoon five years earlier when, following the ecumenical service and blessing of the house, I had gone into the chapel and lay on the floor looking up at the ceiling, feeling a wave of energy and incredulity, like a sailor setting out on a sail across the ocean, excited that we had finally shoved off from shore and were embarked on this audacious voyage.

And now I felt as though I had just been informed that a close friend or family member had died. I sat there, numbly trying to comprehend what had just transpired. Before me I saw a logistic nightmare of leaving this place and finding another in the several months remaining before my own departure, all the while searching for a successor who might not even have the benefit of knowing what the new location would be.

Neither did I relish the thought of bringing this news to our staff. In August, I had the onerous task of going to them with the news, "Guess what? I'm going." And now, six months later, I was in a position of having to bring them the news, "Guess what? We're *all* going!" This was a double whammy. Now *their* jobs and, in some cases, place of residence were on the line. This was what, in pastoral terms, is called "a complicated grieving process."

"It's all going," I thought as I sat in the chapel. "Maybe to another place, in another expression. Maybe nowhere. Maybe it's finished." As T. S. Elliot says in his *Four Quartets*: "For us, there is only the trying. The rest is not our business" (from "East

Coker"). "The rest is prayer, observance, discipline, thought, and action" (from "The Dry Salvages").

Two weeks later, while on a day away skiing, I had a perceptual shift while riding up Mount Mansfield in Vermont in the cabin of a gondola car. All these years I had been saying, "Lord, Unitas is *your* project. I'm just an instrument to serve it." Like curtains being drawn back, all of a sudden the light of insight poured in: *Unitas* is not your project, and we the instruments to serve it. *We* are your project, and Unitas has been an instrument in your hand to serve your work in *us!* Whether Unitas stays or goes is not the question for each of our souls. The question is: Have I followed my deepest desire in doing this? Being able to answer "yes!" to this is what matters most of all for each of us. Have I discovered who I am in doing this, and have I been true to my Self? Has this been my dharma work?

The word *dharma* means many things, but its underlying sense is "that which supports." On a personal level, it implies support from within. On a larger scale, it refers to an integrity and harmony in the universe that cannot be disturbed without courting disaster. When you know who you are and are living your call fully, you *are* "supported from within," you *are* living from integrity and in harmony with the universe. You can *feel* it in your body.

I saw that if, through our engagement in a particular work, we discover who we are in doing it and have been true to our deepest selves, then it has all been worth it. If what we have been involved in fails in one place, we'll do it again in another place, in another expression. The enduringness of the expression of that work is not what matters most. As Keats said of his writing: "If all my poetry, written during the hours of night, should evaporate in the morning and I have nothing to show for it—still, I must write. It is who I am!"

When we are "on the rails" of our calling, of our dharma work, we are already there. We have already arrived. We are doing what we should be doing in the universe. And if we have to stop doing it in one place, we'll just move to a new place and continue doing it there. It's not the *place* that's important.

That night, in our life-sharing circle, I shared this insight with the other residents. They found it a liberating shift of perspective as well. Each of us in our own way could affirm: "I have been following my deepest passion in doing this, and I have been true to that. In so doing, I have discovered more of who I am. Whatever is in our future, we must be true to this and find expression for it in a new place."

In the ensuing months, we found a new director and a new place. On the night before I left, there was a great potluck party with Irish dancing on the terrace under the stars. The board and staff gave me a snazzy pair of roller blades for Central Park in midtown Manhattan, my new home.

"Fully engaged, but ready to let go," my theme throughout the year, was my theme to the final hour. The following day, my last three hours were spent in negotiating an agreement for Unitas's new home.[1] When I came back to the house, I joined the others one last time in the chapel for meditation, and over supper shared the good news with the staff of the settlement on the new location. They followed me out to the driveway where we anointed each other with oil and tears as a final commissioning to service. Then I got in my U-Haul and pointed it in the direction of New York City.

10
Relinquish the Fruits

One of the richest resources I have found in working with the theme of letting go of results is the Bhagavad Gita ("The Song of the Lord"), "India's most important gift to the world."[1] Once I stepped over the line and committed to the Unitas project, the Gita's teaching on relinquishing the fruits and selfless service stood like a lighthouse along rocky shores. Of course, I never managed to fully live it, but it was constantly there like a beacon in the fog, reminding me of where not to go.

In the early part of the first millennium B.C.E., the seers of ancient India analyzed their awareness of human experience to see if anything in it was absolute. Their findings can be summarized in three statements that Aldous Huxley, following Spinoza, termed the Perennial Philosophy because they appear in every age and civilization: (1) there is an infinite, changeless reality beneath the world of change; (2) this same reality lies at the core of every human personality; (3) the purpose of life is to discover this reality experientially: that is, to realize God at the heart of one's being while here on earth.[2]

The Gita's characters are Prince Arjuna, a warrior about to go into battle against family and friends to defend his older brother's claim to the ancient throne of their people, and Krishna, Arjuna's charioteer and advisor who, though Arjuna does not know it, is a divine incarnation. Tragically, Arjuna and his brothers must fight, not an alien army, but one that includes their cousins, who have held the kingdom for many years, as well as their revered teachers and elders who guided them when they were young. While Arjuna wants to win the throne for his brother who has endured many wrongs, he balks at the prospect of fighting his own people. Thus, on the morning the great battle is to begin, he turns to Krishna, his friend and spiritual advisor, and asks him the deep questions about life. The Bhagavad Gita is Krishna's answer.

In this dialogue, Arjuna becomes Everyperson, asking the Lord himself, Sri Krishna, the perennial questions about life and death. The Gita is not an external dialogue, but an internal one between the human personality full of questions about the meaning of life and God. The thread running through Krishna's teaching, the essence of the Gita, is renunciation of selfishness in thought, word, and action—a theme common to mystics of every religion. Gandhi's encapsulation of the Gita, his primary guidebook, took only one phrase: selfless action. Work free from any selfish motives.[3]

In chapter 6 we reflected at length on the role of desire in the choices we make. As we have seen, a great deal of attention is given to human desire in Ignatian spirituality. Not surprisingly, it also comes in for careful scrutiny in Hinduism and Buddhist psychology and spirituality. More often than not, in my experience, the teachings of these religions on desire is misunderstood.

There is a general perception that in the Buddha's teaching, for example, all desires are to be eradicated. If such were genuinely the case, one could not live. Desire is the fuel of life. Without it, nothing could be achieved, let alone something as stupendous as Self-realization or enlightenment. Properly understood, desire in Buddhist teaching relates to "thirst," to the fierce, compulsive craving for personal satisfaction that demands to be slaked at any cost, whether to oneself or others. In other words, *selfish* desire. It is akin to what is often called "self-will" in the works of Western mystics: the false self insisting on getting what it wants for its own gratification. *Nirvana* literally means "extinction of thirst."[4]

As we have seen in chapter 1, when we extinguish the cravings of the false self for security, esteem, control and the false self fades from the scene, ego is able to hear the voice of Self and align itself with it in the choices it makes.

In Hinduism, the Gita in effect proposes a spiritual plan for gradually attaining freedom from the bondage of the false self, from self-centered preoccupation and conditioning. The strategy proposed is a mental discipline, for everything depends on one's state of mind. Actions performed without selfish motives run the false self off the road. Selfish motives are its highway. One of Krishna's most oft-repeated instructions to Arjuna is "relinquish the fruits of your actions."

> You have the right to work, but never to the fruit of work. You should never engage in action for the sake of reward, nor should you long for inaction. Perform work in this world, Arjuna, as a man established within himself—without selfish attachments, and alike in success and defeat. (2:47–48)

"Relinquishing the fruits" means letting go of results. The instruction is to give your best to every undertaking without insisting that the results work out the way you want, or without even insisting that what you do be pleasant or not. Each of us has the obligation to act rightly, but what actually comes of our efforts remains out of our control. Mahatma Gandhi explained his understanding of the teaching on detachment from the fruits of one's efforts: "You must not worry whether the desired result follows from your action or not, so long as your motive is pure, your means correct. Really, it means that things will come right in the end if you take care of the means and leave the rest to Him."[5] But "relinquishing the fruits," Gandhi warns,

> in no way means indifference to the result. In regard to every action one must know the result that is expected to follow, the means thereto, and the capacity for it. He who, being thus equipped, is without desire for the result and is yet wholly engrossed in the due fulfillment of the task before him, is said to have renounced the fruits of his actions.[6]

When one acts in such a way, one finds freedom. Whatever comes, success or failure, praise or blame, one feels peaceful within because one has given one's best. Nothing can shake one's courage or break one's will. One will not fall prey to depression or burnout. "Relinquishing the fruits" establishes one's identification with the Self and enables one to engage in tireless service while remaining in inner peace regardless of the outcome. Only the person both utterly detached and utterly dedicated, Gandhi says, is free to enjoy life. It is difficult for the person compulsively attached to the results of action to really enjoy what she does: If things go badly, she feels dejected; if things go well, she looks over her shoulder for whatever might try to take that success or good feeling from her. Asked to sum up his life in twenty-five words or less, Gandhi replied, "I can do it in three: renounce and enjoy."

Krishna explains to Arjuna the path to inner freedom and peace of heart in these words:

> Better indeed is knowledge than mechanical practice. Better than knowledge is meditation. But better still is surrender of attachment to results, because there follows immediate peace.
>
> That one I love who is incapable of ill will, who is friendly and compassionate. Living beyond the reach of *I* and *mine* and of pleasure and pain, patient, contented, self-controlled, firm in faith, with all his heart and all his mind given to me—with such a one I am in love.
>
> Not agitating the world or by it agitated, he stands above the sway of elation, competition, and fear: he is my beloved.
>
> He is detached, pure, efficient, impartial, never anxious, selfless in all his undertakings; he is my devotee, very dear to me.
>
> He is dear to me who runs not after the pleasant or away from the painful, grieves not, lusts not, but lets things come and go as they happen.
>
> That devotee who looks upon friend and foe with equal regard, who is not buoyed up by praise nor cast down by blame, alike in heat and cold, pleasure and pain, free from selfish attachments, the same in honor and dishonor, quiet, ever full, in harmony everywhere, firm in faith—such a one is dear to me. (12:12–19)

This is a high teaching! Our response in reading it may well be: Who could ever live like that? The life and teachings of Jesus and the Christian mystics are no less demanding.

The Teaching and Example of Jesus

When the sincere young man asked Jesus "What must I do to gain eternal life?", Jesus did not provide a comfortable and easy reply: "Go. Sell everything you have and give it to the poor. And then come, follow me" (Matt 19:21). The young man had a big question—how can I live more fully and deeply?—and he got a bigger answer than he bargained for: "Renounce and enjoy." Jesus could see that his investments were the place where he had to make a break for life. The Spanish mystic John of the Cross said, with reference to attachments, "it makes little difference whether a bird is tied by a thin thread or by a cord. For even if tied by a thread, the bird will be prevented from taking off, just as surely as if it were tied by a cord."[7]

I cannot think of a more dramatic example of relinquishing the fruits of all that one has worked for than Jesus' final journey to Jerusalem, knowing that he was a wanted man there. He was compelled from within to walk into the lion's den with nothing more than a profound trust in God. He didn't know the details of what lay ahead, but he trusted his Father to sustain him and ultimately deliver him as it unfolded. He provided an example for everyone who is sent in his name: be willing to sow seeds and leave the results to God. That is the essence of what it means to relinquish the fruits.

Matthew's description of him in the garden of Gethsemane ("agitated, deeply grieved even to death" [Matt 26:38]), as well as Luke's ("In his anguish he prayed more earnestly and his sweat became like great drops of blood falling down on the ground" [Luke 22:44]), are sober reminders that "letting go" costs dearly. As much as he sought human comfort and support, there was none to be found: His closest disciples lay asleep under a tree in spite of his repeated efforts to rouse them. Johannes Metz asks if we have really understood the impoverishment that Jesus endured in his passion:

> In the poverty of his passion, he had no consolation, no companion angels, no guiding star, no Father in heaven ("My God, My God, why have you forsaken me?"). All he had was his own lonely heart, bravely facing its ordeal even as far as the cross....
>
> Everything was taken from him during the passion, even the love that drove him to the cross. No longer did he savor his own love, no longer did he feel any spark of enthusiasm. His heart gave out and a feeling of utter helplessness came over him. Truly, he emptied himself (Phil 2:7). The Son of Man reached his destiny, stretched taut between a despising earth that had rejected him and a faceless heaven....Jesus paid the price of futility. He became utterly poor....And the legacy of his total commitment to humankind, the proof of his fidelity to our poverty, is the cross....It is the sign that one man remained true to his humanity, that he accepted it in full obedience.[8]

While on a retreat during my college years, the preacher held up a cross and said to us students: "You're not old enough yet to be able to appreciate what this is all about, but some day you will be." I'm only now getting to that age where understanding is starting to come. After I left Unitas, I read through all my journals, from the time of receiving inspiration for that project in India in 1991, to letting go of it and handing it over in 1999. It left me with a profound, cumulative sense of how *difficult* it had all been. Every step of the way. Nothing came easy. And yet, there was joy in it—the infallible sign of the Spirit's presence.

It was at that point that I elected to make a forty-day retreat. "The cross Jesus gives is manageable," my retreat director would say. "His cross is truth—his truth for my life. It's *my* cross that's heavy. *My* truth for my life. 'What are you doing with that one?' Jesus asks. 'I didn't give you that one. My yoke is easy and my burden is light.'" Through the struggles of those years, I learned more about the cross, surrender, and trust than during any other period of my life. There were wounds, but the wounds were life-giving.

I am still too close to that experience to know how the Lord will use in life-giving ways in my future ministry what I lived and learned at Unitas. But I believe that the faith vision and the Holy Spirit will reveal to me ever more clearly with the passing of time how God was working in my life through *both* the inspiration to start it *and* the call to leave it. When we are given to see how the place of our "dying," of our "letting go," is also the place of our blessing, we are, with Thomas, putting our fingers in the hands and side of Christ and answering, "My Lord and my God!" For only God could take wounds and turn them into the place of our healing; only God could take a letting-go and turn it into a filling-up; only God could take death and turn it into fuller life.

It wasn't just the words my retreat director, John Govan, S.J., spoke to me; he himself was a living word for me. Diagnosed in his early thirties to have a brain tumor, he had two operations, after each of which he had to relearn how to use his motor skills. For the period of a few years he was not able even to read. When we look upon such occurrences with the "world vision," all we can see are wasted years, and we shake our heads in sadness and compassion for the person who is living through it. But when we look with the faith vision, we see that through those trying experiences God was writing spiritual wisdom on the person's heart.

Today, he is a sought-after retreat director and teaches university courses on the mystics. When he teaches and preaches, one seldom sees him using notes, because he is speaking out of heart knowledge, out of what he knows through his own personal experience and integration. He has been through the dark tunnel of "knowing I don't know," of dying to autonomy, control, self-sufficiency. The place of his "wound," of his "letting go" and living in trust, now takes on the aura of a special place of blessing in his present ministry that is life-giving for others.

When we are able and willing to persevere in a process of unknowing, of relinquishing the fruits and going forward in trust, God will teach us, if we are willing to wait, to be "born from above." It takes place through a process of being attentive to what we are experiencing in our lives. It's not about head knowledge but heart knowledge. It's about letting God use the experience of our lives to write certain understandings on our hearts. When our faith in God and love for Jesus are strong enough to hold us on the path, we are taught by God in a personal way. We are living then as pilgrims, growing in trust, and God is becoming our only foundation. The conversion process to Christian maturity can only happen when we admit we do not know. The knowledge we have from the world is being replaced by the knowledge that God gives us in Christ. The Holy Spirit is writing the teaching in our hearts. "Blessed are those who have not seen and yet have come to believe" (John 20:29).

In one of his post-resurrection appearances, Jesus appears on the beach while the apostles are fishing (John 21:1–17). Peter and several of the others, fishermen by trade, have been up all night and have caught nothing. Then the stranger on the beach yells out to them to throw the net over on the other side of the boat. When they do and bring it up, it is so full of fish they cannot bring the net into the boat. While Peter has his hands full with the fruits of the sea, suddenly John exclaims: "It is the Lord!" And though he has been up all night with nothing to show for it and is now struggling with a net bursting with fish, Peter lets go of the net, jumps out of the other side of the boat, and starts swimming for shore.

In contemplating this wonderful passage of scripture, I freeze the frame when Peter is in midair between the boat and the water and I just look at it for a long time. *That's* what I want: the kind of heart relationship with the Lord in which no matter what boat I'm in—a ministerial occupation or a favorite pastime—when there's an indication the Lord is beckoning to me from somewhere else, I'm ready to let go of the net—to relinquish the fruits—and to jump over the other side and start swimming. You have to know in looking at that scene that there is a very special heart relationship between the one in the water and the one on the shore. It is love that gives such freedom, love that enables us to relinquish the fruits in the net we were holding and see only the one standing on the beach.

11
The Paschal Mystery: Through Death to New Life

The recurring motif of Christian faith is that the passageway to new life is an experience of dying, of letting go. It's called the paschal mystery. "Paschal" comes from the Greek *pascha* and the Hebrew *pesach*, or Passover, referring to the experience of the Israelites passing over from bondage in Egypt to new life as a people in a promised land. For all our mythology around that experience, we can be sure that for the people who lived the exodus, it was painfully concrete and specific.

The same is true when we find the imprint of the paschal mystery on our lives. It is not an invisible stamp on the hand like one receives in passing through the turnstile at an amusement park, to come clear only under the celestial spotlight of heaven's gatekeeper when we exit this life. The passage to new life starts with some concrete decision—to mark out more quality time with one's spouse; to see your boss about abusive ways of relating among the employees; to talk with your son or daughter about that delicate subject you have both been avoiding; to reach out to an "enemy"; to get up a half hour earlier in the morning and begin meditating; to give a few months of your life to a humanitarian project. Jesus' invitation to us is always an invitation to more and fuller life: "I came that they may have life, and have it abundantly" (John 10:10).

But the death and resurrection of Jesus does more than inspire us to take the particular step that may lead to more abundant life. His cross and resurrection reveal the secret of all aliveness, his and ours: Life is renewed through the habitual laying down of life. "Very truly I tell you, unless a grain of wheat falls into the earth and dies, it remains just a single grain; but if it dies, it bears much fruit" (John 12:24). New life through dying. This is the reality of things. This deep mystery is certainly writ large for us in the events of Jesus' final days, but just so we don't miss it, God has also written it into the natural world all around us. The acorn carries the tremendous potential within itself of a towering oak tree, but unless its shell cracks open and disintegrates, its full potential will never be realized. The caterpillar crawls into its tomblike chrysalis and metamorphoses into something both in continuity with the old and yet new and more beautiful: a butterfly. From the frozen ground and barren trees of winter, flowers and new leaves burst forth. No dying, no new life. No emptying, no being filled. Everywhere in the universe it is written: *Life comes through dying.* It is the principle of all existence.

It pertains to the universe of human relations as well. What parent has not lived a "letting go" similar to the one described by Glenda Carline in this humorous, poignant essay entitled "Shopping with the Blue-Haired Boy," and related in her family newsletter to friends.

The autumn moved me into a new season of my life. I was soon to discover that being the mother of a junior high school boy had its own pattern of weather and color. He walked through the doors into his junior high school a boy,

and emerged later that same day a teenager. Within a fort-
night the changes occurring within him sought an external
visible expression.

"I want to dye my hair blue" he said with conviction.
Not words this mother anticipated hearing for her twelve-
year-old boy or words that would propel any parent out the
door to the drugstore in search of blue dye. Perhaps talking
about this desire for blue hair would abate the need to actually make it so. But his passion for blue grew and before
long he had secured the help of his grandma to acquire the
needed hair fudge from a punk hair style shop on trendy
Whyte Avenue. A few hours at Grandma's house and his
transformation was made. The blond locks of his childhood, not accented with a soft blue hue common amongst
elderly women, but stained a blue that earned him the
nickname of "blueberry" and "smurf" amongst his peers.
He was ecstatic.

We quickly earned our stripes as junior high parents.
The first Sunday to church with the blue-haired boy.
Awards night with the blue-haired boy; in the stands watching his first-ever indoor soccer game, the parents of "the
blue-haired boy."

Soon came the shopping trip. It seemed the all-season
black sweatpants he had made his personal uniform
throughout elementary school had to go. So off we went,
the blue-haired boy and I, in search of the coveted cargo
pants. From store to store we trudged. His focus on the
very particular style of cargo pant—a style only he could
accurately identify. My focus was a reasonable price range
that fit the family budget. It seemed that his "direct hits"

on style completely missed the target for my budget. And conversely, my enthusiasm over a "find" that met the budget, apparently completely missed out on the fashion statement.

Until, as if by magic, we stumbled upon the sale rack of assorted and mismatched youth clothing. BINGO. The cargos fit the budget and the fashion requirements. Now if they would only fit the boy. He took them into the change room, a renewed sense of bounce in his step that had diminished on the path through the last twelve shops. He emerged from the change room with a bright smile. "They're perfect, Mom!" My smile of relief faded as I looked at the abundance of fabric he had gripped in one hand to hold the garment in place and the two puddles of cloth around his feet. "Could you shorten them a bit?" he tried to convince me. "Maybe move the button over, too," he added. Actually if he had unzipped the fly, he could have wrapped one flap completely around his waist and the button would have been in just about the right spot. He begged and pleaded, and finally the sale tag flapping off the waist band convinced me to proceed to the sales desk.

As we walked together through the mall with a sense of accomplishment, he kept a suitable junior high distance, occasionally glancing at his own image in the glass of the shop fronts. I watched him. This same person who had offered me his hand to hold as we walked in days gone by now kept both stuffed in his oversized pant pockets. This same person, who had to be dragged and tricked to flatten the "rooster" out of his matted hair, now kept a comb at hand and sought out his reflection in the storefront glass.

This was a new season for me. And as the autumn trees let go their leaves, I too had to let go of my son, the boy, and make space for the emerging youth.

These instances of "letting go" fill our daily living, most consistently in our struggle to let go of yesterday, of the past. Whether it's turning twenty-one, thirty, fifty, or seventy-five. Whether it's losing our health or our hair, our money or our memory, a person we love or a possession we prize. The Paschal Mystery of Christ says: Let go of where your security once lay. Trust that new life will be given.

Whether it's being fired or retired, divorced or disabled, whether it's a change of life or a change of pace—the Paschal Mystery of Christ says: Do not cling to what once was but is no more. Make an act of faith that a new day will dawn. No dying, no new life. No emptying, no being filled.

Whenever we are faced in any way with a form of "dying" or "letting go," the Paschal Mystery of Christ is there to shape our perception of what is happening, and to give an affirming stamp to our hope that out of this "death" will come new life and growth.

So wherever or whatever or with whomever we've been, we dare not cling. We have to move on. And letting go is a dying. But only by dying will we rise to fresh life. Only by letting go of yesterday will we open ourselves to tomorrow, where the seeds of fresh life await us.

Questions That Lead to Life

Once while leading a retreat in Maryland, I listened to one of the participants, Gretchen Hannon, talk about her daughter's death. I knew it had been traumatic for her, and when she said "my life has a depth and richness it never had before Lisa's death," I wondered if I had heard her correctly. I asked her if she would elaborate, and this is what she shared:

Lisa was twenty-four when she died. She had graduated from the University of Virginia in December, 1993, and was working toward getting a job in Africa where she wanted to live and do work in humanitarian aid. She had already spent a year there between her sophomore and junior years in college, teaching in a small village, Kitale, in northern Kenya. She taught boys between the ages of fifteen and twenty-five (she didn't admit to them her age of twenty.) She taught English, built a library with friends and family contributing books, and led a Boy Scout troop in drama. Her attachment to Africa went back to having been born in Nairobi and living her first five years in Kenya and Tanzania.

She died in a car accident. She had been leading a 400-person mission with the Virginia search and rescue effort for a missing five-year-old boy in the Shenandoah Mountains. She had been on duty for thirty-six hours, had been relieved, and was driving home on a sunny Tuesday morning less than twenty minutes from the rescue site when she fell asleep behind the wheel of her truck. It hit a tree. She was alone. It was May 3, 1994.

How do I describe how I came from a place of terrible grief to a place of deep blessing? Almost two years after Lisa died, I was stuck in my grief. I found I was unable to converse without crying. Somehow I knew I needed to go deeper into the pain to get through it, yet I'd experienced so much I didn't want to endure more, and I was unable to work with it constructively myself. So one of my friends suggested the name of someone who might help me. I called her—sobbing incoherently on the phone—and though she was booked for two years, she said she'd see me.

Nina was what I would call a spiritual intuitive. The first time we met, she simply invited me to breathe deeply, close my eyes and say what my body was feeling. She said she trusted that what I said would be what needed to be said. No need to go into a lot of words. Almost immediately I felt Lisa being present to me as a guide, encouraging me on this journey. What I experienced was light, not pain. And that has been so since.

I continued to work with Nina for the next year and a half. I have learned to trust my body-mind and my feelings to get in touch with places otherwise unavailable to me, and now I am learning to trust my intuitive wisdom. Instead of a journey, it's more an unfolding. I am still; the movement is within. The grief gave me access. I have now come to call it the Gift of Grief. It seems to be a gift that continues to open and reveal itself. I am attentive to reoccurring waves of grief. I don't avoid, but go into, the feelings offered me in the present moment. I've always "worked from the heart," but this has brought me to a new level of being honest within myself.

I frequently think how much Lisa loved life. Am I living mine? Am I being as clear in my choices as she was in hers? Am I speaking my authentic voice, as she taught me to do? Am I greeting each day with the verve and vigor that defined her energy? Am I caring for others in a way that defined how she lived her life?

Two and a half years ago, my elder daughter, Kimberly, asked if I would work with her in her business. It is a part of this story because Kimberly and I are aware that it is also a gift from Lisa. If she were alive, we probably wouldn't be working this way together. Our energy patterns and relationships would be different. Working with Kimberly is truly a blessing. To work together with deep respect and love is wonderful! We've always been close as a family (three children born within three years of each other, living overseas and depending on each other), but now the relationship is even closer.

When we are standing in the middle of an experience of loss, we come face to face with a deep truth: Nothing is mine. All can disappear. And then come the questions which lead to life. They are the very questions that Gretchen enunciated: Am I *living* my life? Am I being clear in my choices? Am I speaking from my authentic voice? Am I caring for others?

The experience of loss is real. It is painful. The promise in it is that it will push us to a new level of maturity and faith. In working with her grief following her daughter's death, Gretchen related how she learned to "go into" her feelings rather than to avoid them. This, too, is an important part of "letting go"—not to resist the feelings that come up, but to allow oneself to experience them, to ride the wave of sadness, of nostalgia, of loneliness like a surfer, to flow with the emotional current rather than trying to paddle upstream against it. Resisted, the emotions dam up and block the flow of energy within, but when allowed to flow they eventually move through like a series of large waves, finally giving way to calm water once again. The presence of friends or family or a counselor let us know, as Nina did for Gretchen, that we are not alone in the midst of the turbulent waters, but supported and carried by the love and care of others.

Full Catastrophe Living

In his book, *Full Catastrophe Living*, John Kabat-Zinn reflects that it is not easy to find a word or phrase that really captures the broad range of experiences in life that cause us distress and pain and that promote in us an underlying sense of fear, insecurity, and loss of control.

What could we possibly call the sum total of our vulnerabilities and inadequacies, our limitations and weaknesses as people, the illnesses and injuries and disabilities we may have to live with, the personal defeats and failures we have felt or fear in the future, the injustices or exploitations we suffer or fear, the losses of people we love and of our bodies sooner or later: It would have to be a metaphor that would not be maudlin, something that would also convey the understanding that it is not a disaster to be alive just because we feel fear and we suffer; it would have to convey the understanding that there is joy as well as suffering, hope as well as despair, calm as well as agitation, love as well as hatred, health as well as illness.[1]

In looking for such a word or phrase, Kabat-Zinn kept coming back to a line from the movie *Zorba the Greek* in which Zorba's young companion asks him if he has ever been married. "Am I not a man?" Zorba replies. "Of course I've been married. Wife, house, kids, everything…the full catastrophe!"

Catastrophe here does not mean disaster, and Zorba was not lamenting being married or having children. Rather, his response embodies a supreme appreciation for the richness of life and the inevitability of all its dilemmas, sorrows, tragedies, and ironies. "The full catastrophe" summarizes the poignant enormity of our life experience—crises and disaster, and all the big and little things that go wrong and that add up. The expression reminds us that everything we think is permanent is really only temporary and constantly in flux: our ideas, opinions, relationships, jobs, possessions, creations, bodies—everything! The phrase captures something positive about the human spirit's ability to come to grips with what is most trying in life and to find within it the space to grow in wisdom and strength. "There is not one person on the planet," postulates Kabat-Zinn, "who does not have his or her version of the full catastrophe."[2]

The Experience of Loss

Loss is a far more encompassing theme in our lives than we realize. We deal with it constantly in the loss of power or position, spouse or friends, country or school, limbs and legacies. Included in our losses are dreams, hopes, expectations, illusions of freedom and security, to say nothing of the illusions of our own eternal youth, health, and immortality. These losses are unavoidable and inexorable. *And* they are the beginning of wisdom, the beginning of hopeful change. The road to human development is paved with the experience of letting go. Throughout our life we grow by giving up. The growth comes from responding to these losses in constructive ways. Peaceful acceptance leads to the possibility of creative growth, whereas resentment and resistance leads to bitterness, cynicism, and despair.[3]

While leading a retreat in Edmonton, Alberta, I met Faith Nostbakken. We had some good conversations, and have stayed in communication. People like Faith are my teachers. You will understand why after learning something of her story.

There are top and bottom layers to my story. The bottom layer is that for the past ten and a half years I've been living with an illness known as Chronic Fatigue Syndrome or Chronic Fatigue and Immune Dysfunction Syndrome or Myalgic Encephalomyelitis—CFS or ME for short. My journey into illness began abruptly on July 25th, 1990, when I came down with a severe respiratory infection that had all the symptoms of mono, although tests for that virus came back negative, so apparently I was suffering from a similar virus, never clearly identified. I thought, in fact, I had a "flu"; I thought it would last a week or two. I had no idea what I was getting into, and I have to say I'm sure glad I didn't. I can't quite imagine knowing then what I know now about how that sudden viral invasion would change my life as the initial infection led to a much more serious condition, a syndrome or disease that is difficult to diagnose, impossible—as yet—to cure, unresponsive to most symptomatic treatments, mysterious beyond understanding, and devastating in its impact on my body, my possibilities for employment and other simple activities, and my sense of self.

Along the way in the past twelve years, I lost so many ways of being me that I tried to foster hope by narrowing my list of expectations. I decided that I could live the rest of my life without certain opportunities and pleasures I had once enjoyed. If I never had an opportunity to run a mile or two again, I could live with that, although I loved to run. If I never had a chance to go camping and climb a mountain again, I could live with that, although they had been summer pleasures from my youth up until a week or two before I first became ill.

But I recognized that there were certain activities that were expressions of who I was—extensions of myself—and I wasn't sure how I would know myself and be myself without them. The list was small (I thought): just three things—teaching, writing, and making music. Well, a few months later, I wasn't teaching anymore, and the probabilities of doing it anytime in the near future looked unlikely. I couldn't sign my signature without agony, so writing was beyond comprehension. And, of all things unexpected, I lost my voice so not only couldn't I converse and communicate well, I couldn't sing, which was the only music-making left to me when weakness and then pain compelled me to give up the piano, organ, flute, recorder, and guitar years before. The bare essentials that I had put in my hope chest were gone, and so when I opened the lid, it looked completely empty. That's what forced the question about whether hope was hanging on or letting go.

In order to start hoping again, I recognized the need to relinquish my short list because hanging onto those three activities when they were no longer happening in me and through me was leading me to a place of despair, and I knew that couldn't be the work of true hope. I had to open one hand and let go completely. And with the other hand, I had to hang on for dear life to dear life and to my belief that I belonged to a God who loved me. Whatever that meant, I needed to believe it.

It wasn't an easy task, letting go completely. As I can recall, it happened over a period of months and probably more like years because I had—and still have—this impulse to keep grabbing back again what I want and think I need, and, in doing so, losing my grip on the far more open-ended hope promised by the God who loves me. I may be doing this with my hands at different times under different circumstances for the rest of my life. But I keep coming across words of wisdom or encouragement to draw me back to the paradox—the apparent contradiction—of needing simultaneously to hang on and to let go. Every once in while I looked at my hands, at the open palms and fingers trembling with weakness, alternatively opening and closing them, contemplating the options: to hang on or to let go. When an answer came—and it's the answer I still carry with me today—I discovered that it was the word "both." What is hope? It is hanging on and letting go, and on any given day or at any given period in my life, what I need to hang onto and what I need to let go of may change slightly, but I sensed—and still do—an awareness of the need to do both.

I struggled to focus on the Giver rather than the gifts, and somehow to be willing to wait without even being able to preoccupy myself with some kind of simple activity to make the waiting more bearable. Strangely enough, or perhaps not strangely at all, what was happening in the silence and solitude during that period of dark shadows without much activity or responsibility is that God drew me close in a way I have never known or experienced God's presence before, and began communicating with me in the conversation of prayer as I had never experienced it before. And much of what happened between us during that time planted life-changing seeds for what I've chosen to call "the top layer of the story." I know God is actively engaged in shaping the top layer of my story from now into eternity and that every step along the way matters.

I remember saying once, "Life itself is gift, and every-thing else is bonus." I have had enough of the extras pared down in my life for a short or long term that I am much better at celebrating what comes as bonus than I used to be. A good night's sleep? Bonus! A good meal that I can eat and that my body accepts as nourishment? Bonus! The ability to sign my name or write a grocery list—or maybe even a book—or two? Bonus! The voice to say "hello" and maybe even much more than that? Oh, glorious bonus! All these words! The ability to walk more than a short distance with-out pain even if I can't do a few blocks or run miles? Bonus! A roof over my head and enough money for rent? Bonus! Employment and a paycheck, too? Ah, that would really be a bonus; I can just imagine. Family and friends who care? Just about the best bonus of all! All the good people who enter into and share my life and let me enter into and share theirs. Bonus! The abundant life!

Would I have thought that way if it had been easy to take all the givens for granted from day one until now? I don't know and partly I doubt it but God works with what we have, not what we don't have. And even though I also don't think God was at all instrumental in the onset of my illness or any part of it, I do believe God is always willing to write the top layer of the story above the bottom layer. And one of the beautiful parts of the top layer that might be different if the bottom layer were also different is that God has been transforming my way of seeing for the better. The Divine Seer has improved my sight to notice all the gifts given—in sickness or in health—from the simplest to the most elaborate, from the tiniest to the grandest, from the most ordinary to the utterly extravagant. In fact, about that whole top layer of the story, I say, "Bonus!"

I know a wholeness that has been growing through my illness in a way that I never imagined experiencing when I was well. I am living a story way bigger than I am. When I shared this with a wise counselor, she responded, "I think everybody has stories bigger than they are." And I believe she's right. We all do; we just don't all recognize it. We aren't in the practice of looking for it. Some of us are afraid to see it. And not everybody has the same ability to find the words to express it. But we all have stories bigger than we are—a wonderful promise or a terrifying challenge, depending on the day, and on the way that faith and hope fill the insides of those stories.[4]

Faith would be the first to attest that the balance between "letting go" and "hanging on" needs constant retuning. But when she speaks out of her experience about hanging on ("for dear life to dear life") having a role to play, we intuit the truthfulness of what she witnesses to. Her list of "bonus" items keeps those things fresh for me and prevents me from taking them for granted. But what instructs me most is her awareness of the "top layer," of what God is writing on her heart through the years of this "letting go" process.

I learn many things from Faith, but one of them is how loss offers a crossing-over. Not painless or uncostly, but a crossing over to solidarity with a wider group of people, to a wider perspective from which to judge what has been left behind, to a new experience of creatureliness, or of presence, or of vulnerability, of the gratuity of all that is given and normally taken for granted. I learn from her that if we do not thwart it, loss opens us to new knowledge of ourselves and of others who have lost and lived and learned.

The limitations and losses that mar and mark all our lives shape our identities. Those identities can never be lost. They only blossom into greater integrity and deeper wisdom.

It's All for Keeps

Loss is one of the ultimates of the universe. Yet there is a profound inclination within us to deny its reality. Geophysicist Brian

Swimme talks about how we don't live in a placid universe, but in a universe of great upheaval. The fireball at the beginning of creation was a very violent act. A black hole can suck up hundreds of thousands of stars. But the new galaxies wouldn't have come into being without it. Everything in the universe has its cost. All creativity has a cost. Every new manifestation has an energy requirement. Our universe makes tremendous demands, requires energy, uses it, absorbs it. "The Mass is about God sacrificing for the universe. If God is willing to 'lose' something for the universe, everything else should be willing, too."[5]

Fossil records indicate that a billion species have come into existence. Only ten million are left now. Only one in a hundred have survived. Nature is a vast, violent, unpredictable undertaking, and it's all for keeps. Extinctions are always taking place. The dinosaurs had their day, and now they're gone. To embrace the terror in loss is to be liberated from egotism and selfishness and superficiality.

In the process of evolutionary change, Swimme observes, it helps if the environment is less than ideal, if stress is involved. That is what pushes small groups—the explorers of radical intuition—to new breakthroughs. They explore the way in which their genetic creativity is leading them. In each decision we make, we don't know what we're going to become. But everything we interact with is shaping us for that next step.[6]

When God demands that Moses—who has a price on his head for having killed an Egyptian—return to Egypt, to Pharaoh himself, and boldly demand that the Israelites be set free, Moses' response is: "Who am I that I should go to Pharaoh and lead the Israelites out of Egypt?" God only says, "I will be with you." And then follows one of the scariest passages in the Bible. God tells

Moses that he will be sure that it is God who has called him to this task *only* when it is accomplished.[7]

This is a God that demands great willingness to trust and take risks. At the headwaters of the Judaeo-Christian story is an account in which Abraham, 100 years old, is asked to bind up and lay on an altar of sacrifice the very one through whom the promise was to be realized. In the terse phrase of Genesis 22:1, "God tested Abraham." What was the test? To relinquish the fruits. The literal fruit of his loins, his son, his *only* son, the joy of his life, the answer to his and Sarah's prayer, the one through whom he was to become the father of many nations. "Take your son, your only son Isaac, whom you love, and go to the land of Moriah, and offer him there as a burnt offering on one of the mountains that I shall show you" (22:2).

What we see in Abraham and Moses is that we are called to faithful obedience—not to do something because it will "work" or be popular. As the sign I've seen in various places reads: "God does not call us to be successful but to be faithful." Faith isn't practical or functional; it refuses to be limited by pragmatism. It's a way of standing in the world with a referent beyond.

Additional Time to Be a Witness to Grace

I met Ed Woodman during my first years of ministry at the Ohio State University Newman Center in Columbus. We enjoyed our time together in church as much as on the softball field. Ed went on to become a counseling psychologist in an Ohio high school. We lost touch for several years when I was transferred to Canada, but when Ed surfaced again, he had a story to tell.

In August of 1998 I began an unexpected journey that revealed to me the power of faith and the grace bestowed in response to prayer—my own and others. I was diagnosed with colon cancer. Following the initial diagnosis I went to school to tell my principal that I would be on sick leave for the first semester. I then notified other members of my family as well as friends of my situation. The next day I was driving somewhere and I remember making a silent prayer to God: "Whatever is to happen, just let me be an example of faith to others." The words surfaced in my mind and caught me somewhat by surprise. From that point on I felt remarkably at peace with my situation.

The day for surgery arrived. I recall having other minor surgeries in the past and being quite nervous. But this time I was very calm as they wheeled me to surgery. The family wished me well and they rolled me into the operating room.

A few days later I received the pathology report; the news was not good. Twenty of twenty-two lymph nodes were cancerous. The prognosis was dismal. The oncologist stopped by one afternoon to explain the chemo and radiation regimen I would undergo. When asked if I had any questions, I replied, "No, it is out of my control." The look on his face suggested displeasure. "What I mean," I said, "is that I trust you to do your part. I will keep a positive attitude and do my part, and the rest is up to God." I am not one to be very vocal about my faith, and was somewhat surprised at my own words.

Some weeks later I began my chemo treatments. The recovery was slow and the effects of the chemo and radiation treatments prevented me from venturing out very often, so I spent a lot of time at home. I have long had a devotion to Our Lady of Fatima and have occasionally turned to her in times of difficulty. One day the movie *The Miracle of Our Lady of Fatima* was on TV. I had seen it several times before, but it stirred something in me that caused me to start praying on a daily basis. I thought I was dying.

Treatments ended about seven months later, and the oncologist ordered up a CT scan as a precaution, since my cancer had been so advanced. The results indicated a spot on my liver about the size of a thumb. He indicated my chances of surviving were not good and that my only chance would be surgery. I returned to the surgeon; he said we needed to wait a couple months, after which time he would do another scan. If the cancer hadn't spread I would be a candidate for surgery.

Meanwhile, my friend Kathy asked me if I felt like I had been blessed with a miracle. She revealed that on a recent trip out west she stopped by a chapel known for its miracles and left a prayer petition on my behalf.

After waiting for two months, the PET scan was finally conducted. It would either show the cancer to be contained and operable or show that it had spread and was now terminal. My doctor called and told me he was confused. "I'm looking at your scans" he said, "and there is nothing wrong with you." Not only was I stunned, but I had the impression he was as well. I have had several check-ups since, and on one of those visits I shared my faith experience with him. He told me he had one other patient whose condition was very bad and he gave her no hope of surviving. But, he said, she was a spiritual woman, and five years later she continues to do well. He told me to keep praying.

So my life goes on buoyed by the prayers of family and friends and a faith that grows deeper by the day with gratitude for my many blessings. Each day I give thanks for the gift of my cancer because it set me on a new path in my journey of faith. It was during this journey that I rediscovered a God with whom I had lost touch and a God who has blessed me with additional time to be a witness to his grace and healing power.

As each new evolution in a situation occurs, we just keep going forward with the best lights we have, trusting that our mysterious God is writing straight with crooked lines and that there will be a happy ending. If Ed's doctor had said, "The cancer has spread and we don't feel putting you through an operation will do any good at this point," it wouldn't have meant God was absent. I'm sure Ed would have felt God's presence with him in either scenario. As he had earlier told the doctor, "It's in God's hands." He was going to do his part and trusted that the doctor would do the same, but as for the results, he let them go. In the end, his response to the situation is simply "God has blessed me with additional time to be a witness to his grace and healing power." What more can any of us say each day as we get out of bed in the morning? God has given me another day to see the light, to walk in the light, and to share it with others. God has given me additional time to be a witness to grace.

In meditating on the first joyful mystery of the rosary, the annunciation of the angel Gabriel to Mary that she was to be the mother of the Son of the Most High, Mary's anxious, fearful, and deeply troubled response (Luke 1:29, 30) was probably an object lesson for Ed. We have a tendency to think that faith leaves no room for doubt. But a mature faith must confront the reality of doubt. Daily we experience trials that cause us to question. It is at the very places of our doubt that faith is made real and strong. The conviction that God is in it with us—that if we embrace this loss, this dying, in trust, God will use everything that happens to redeem our loss and turn it into gold—is at the very heart of Christian faith. It's called the Paschal Mystery.

One of the things that impresses me about Ed's story is that he looked for God in the dark. When we face sickness, pain, suffering, loss, or uncertainty, it's like trying to see in the dark. Many of us tend to look for God only in places where there is light. We need a way of seeing in the dark. The cross of Christ provides it. Looking at life from the angle of the cross is like using night-vision field glasses. It lets us see Presence in silence, power in weakness, and light in darkness. The cross of Christ enables us to live in hope with suffering and loss, because it reveals to us that we do not suffer alone or in vain. It enables us to see that though we may not be rescued from the circumstances of our suffering, we will be redeemed.

Seeing in the Dark

During a parish mission in Minneapolis, I met a man who gave new meaning to the image of "seeing in the dark." His name is Peter McKenna. In 1945 Peter was in an antitank squadron in Germany during World War II. They were fired upon, and a shell fragment hit the shell he was holding. It exploded in his hands. The field doctor's cursory diagnosis was: face shot off, both arms fractured, left hand mutilated with thumb and forefinger dangling, both eyes burned out.

The fingers were amputated, the arms eventually healed, and for one year the plastic surgeon rebuilt Peter's face. He needed nose, lips, eyelids, eyebrows, and new facial tissue.

During his two subsequent years in a Veteran's hospital he was cared for by Mary John, his nurse. Their relationship grew, and in 1949 they married. They had nine children, who have given them sixteen grandchildren and four great-grandchildren. But Peter, whose eyes were gone forever, has never seen his wife, his children, or his grandchildren.

Along the way, however, Peter learned to "see in the dark." He could not see his wife and children with his physical eyes, but with the eyes of his soul he clearly discerned their loving and enabling presence. So it is with the Christian in every experience of transition, of letting go, of loss, of dying—in short, in every experience of the cross. Through the night-vision field glasses of faith, one "sees in the dark" God's loving and supportive presence.

During the mission, I watched Peter come into church every day on Mary's arm, and one day after the service I asked them to share their story with me. Peter ended it with words I will never forget: "I'd like to find the German soldier that shot me and thank him. Bringing Mary into my life was the best thing that ever happened to me. If I had to do it all over again, I would."

What a powerful testimony to the mystery of the cross: that God is present to us and actively assisting us in the midst of tragedy, suffering, and death, drawing good out of evil, salvation out of suffering, and new life out of death.

Christ on the cross reveals to us that there is now no area of life that falls outside the presence and activity of God. That is liberating news for faint hearts. Christians venerate the cross on Good Friday not as an instrument of torture, but as a trophy of victory. In its shadow, we find new courage to confront our losses and to live our letting-go's. In the shadow of the cross, we contemplate the Paschal Mystery of Christ: through death to new life.

Christian baptism is meant to convey precisely this: down into the waters of death, and up and out into newness of life. The life is his, and in that mystical bond with him, we are committed to the pattern of dying and rising in our living, in our decisions, in our relationships, in our careers, in our vocations. Our baptismal calling to be Christ in the world is not a career option but a calling, and sometimes the conditions aren't the ones we would have chosen for ourselves. The irony is that what God calls us to is always life-giving. In symbolic terms, the paths we are invited to leave behind give way to paths of greater possibility. The doors we are urged to close are smaller than the doors that open before us. The dwelling we are asked to vacate makes way for mansions of inestimable size and value. God continually invites us to greater consciousness, to greater freedom, and to more opportunities for loving.[8]

In the process of writing this book, I became conscious that many of the stories provided by people in it emerged from experiences of suffering. Why was that, I asked myself? I knew I hadn't set out to collect stories of suffering as such. What had happened, rather, is that as I listened to people's stories, I was drawn by the wisdom and insight in them. Only after bringing a number of stories together and looking at them did the pattern become apparent. The wisdom, the new life and insight, flowed from the dying, the letting-go. I take that as a confirmation of the paschal mystery. The wisdom that comes from suffering responded to in hope and faith is a reflection of the mystery of the cross and the resurrection at work in the world.

Here is the interpretive key for all our deaths and losses: from the failure of an exam to the breakup with a lover; from seeing one's child leave home for the first time to letting go of a childish faith; from moving house to the loss of a job; from disablement to retirement. Cling to what you have at that moment and you are lost. Unclench your grasp and open your hands to receive what life offers you in the new, fresh moment, and you are on the path to life.[9] Renounce and enjoy. Relinquish the fruits. Die and Rise.

One Thing More

I recognize these themes at work when I get the opportunity to spend a few days with a friend I don't see very often. There is a little drama that plays itself out at the end of each day. The title is always the same: "One Thing More."

It doesn't matter that the day has been rich and full to overflowing with outdoor activity, stimulating conversation, rich moments of shared silence, heartfelt prayer, and delicious food. The curtain always goes up on this little play called "One Thing

More." One more subject of conversation, one more set of music, one more beer, one more activity or program.

The players come out from the wings of insecurity and fear. They draw their script from the unconscious fears that the end of the day holds: Every little ending signals a bigger ending. Will this be it? Will this be "the end"? Will we ever see each other again? Ever have quality time like this again together?

It is only in demasking the players that we begin to become free of their upsetting and unsettling lines. Enter one: "You are my fear that the future will not be as good as the present." Enter another: "You are my insecurity that life or Providence will not provide me with another with whom I can share something of what I have shared with you."

It is a crisis of confidence at the end of each day. *And,* it is our richest field of spiritual practice. There where the challenge lies, the greatest potential for growth is found. Inner, spiritual freedom is strengthened and its terrain broadened when we become aware of what we cling to and consciously let it go. When we release it into the air like a dove opening its wings and taking flight, rather than clutching it to our breast, we make an act of faith in the abundance of God's love manifesting in our lives in unimaginable ways at every turn of the road. We put "scarcity thinking" behind us. We laugh the players of fear and insecurity from the stage and tell them their script is old and empty.

It is an ongoing struggle, a constant asceticism. I am constantly uncovering subtle efforts within me to secure the future. If my friend and I have three days together, by the middle of the second day I am already working on plans in my mind for "next year." I have to constantly bring myself back to the gift given in the present moment and trust that from God's abundance the gift that is given this way now will be given again in other ways then. There is no end to unhooking from that grasping movement of the mind. No end to unlocking the hoarding instincts of the heart.

The road to spiritual freedom, to freedom from our fears of being left alone with no one to love and care for us, is long. It is a road covered step by step, one act of letting go after another, an hour-by-hour act of faith in God's abundance, ability, and desire to provide for all our needs in every moment.

My friends and I are learning to recognize the onset of the daily rendition of "One Thing More," to name it as soon as the curtain goes up, and to gently deny its little ploys. When we do, the genre shifts from tragedy to comedy, and the script is changed from one based on insecurity and fear to one based on humor, confidence, and trust.

If you and I can learn the "letting-go reflex" from the small occasions that daily come to us, then when the Big Letting-Go arrives, we will face it with familiarity and peace. Those who have truly lived are free to die. Those who have learned to relinquish the fruits and leave results to God are free to live.

When we know who we are, discern our call and respond to it fully by living from our gifts, and let go of results, we're free to respond with passion and energy to what life sets before us right here, right now.

Reflection Questions

A. Reflect on your losses, whether in terms of power or position, spouse or friends, health or hair, money or memory, material possessions or legacies.

B. Did you grow by giving up? Did new life come through "dying"/letting go? If sometimes "yes" and sometimes "no," was there any difference in your own approach or attitude that may have influenced the eventual outcome?

C. What role did faith play in the way you lived through these experiences of "letting go"?

Step Four

Daily Rededicate Your Life to God

Spiritual Freedom

I want to be like
that rooster
made of metal
standing alert on one leg
atop a pinnacled roof
stopping between engagements
looking and listening
equipoised
to move in the direction
the breath of God
next blows.

12

Called and Sent

> The disciple is one who is called
> one who first unfolds a delicate blossom
> which then gives birth to a small fruit
> that is allowed to ripen in the sun.
> The apostle is one who is sent
> the mature fruit now ready
> to be picked and offered
> for the nourishment of others.
> Am I ready to be picked?
> Am I ready to be eaten?

All too often those who are sent—apostles—lose their motivation and their fire. They lose touch with the inspiration of their experience of being called. What married person, what member of a religious community or minister of the gospel has not at times lost the fervor of the first years following their commitment and lived through barren stretches of desert? An apostle's way of staying close to his or her desire is to continually go back to the experience of being a disciple, of sitting at the feet of the Lord to listen and learn and fall in love again. That was essentially why I chose to make a retreat between leaving Montreal and beginning a new ministry in New York: to move back into the disciple mode. To stoke up the fire of my experience of being called. To stay close to my heart's deepest desire. To fall in love again. To rededicate myself to God.

An essential prelude to the Exercises is what Ignatius called The First Principle and Foundation. It's his answer to the question: "When you melt it all down, what is life all about?" One of the retreat directors, Sister Karen Doyle, took Ignatius's answer and expressed it from God's point of view:

(Your name), the goal of your life is to live with me forever. I gave you life because I love you. Your response of love allows my life to flow into you without limit.

All the things in this world are my gifts, presented to you so that you can know me more easily and return your love to me more readily.

I want you to appreciate and use all my gifts insofar as they help you develop as a loving person. But if any of my gifts become the center of your life, they displace me and so hinder your growth toward your goal.

In everyday life, then, you must hold yourself in balance before all of my created gifts insofar as you have a choice and are not bound by some obligation. You should not fix your desire on health or sickness, wealth or poverty, success or failure, a long life or a short one. For everything has the potential of calling forth in you a deeper response to your life in me.

Your only desire and one choice should be this: to want and to choose what better leads to my deepening my life in you.

All the themes we have dealt with in the first three sections are there: identity, call, letting go of results. And the final line prefigures the theme of this chapter: Rededicate your life to God.

First- and Secondhand Religion

Every time I read the Gospel of John, what stands out for me is that at every turn of the road Jesus checks in with "Abba," submits his life to him and rededicates himself to serving his purposes in the world. What is more, Jesus invited his followers into that intimate relationship with God that he himself experienced. Surely it was this *experience* of God that lent sovereignty to his voice when he taught: "You have heard it said, but I say…." The God Jesus knew was the compassionate one, not the God of requirements and boundaries. The way of Jesus challenges us to move from "secondhand religion" to "firsthand religion."[1]

We live secondhand religion when our way of being religious is based on believing what we have heard from others. When we think that the Christian life is only about believing what the Bible says or what the doctrines of the church say, we're living with secondhand religion. Firsthand religion consists of a relationship to that which the Bible and the teachings of the church point—the reality we call God. Between the two, there is a perceptive shift, a transformation from living according to what one has *heard*, to *life centered in the Spirit of God*. At the climax of the Book of Job, after he has experienced a dramatic self-disclosure of God, Job provides one of the clearest expressions of this transformation in the Bible: "I had heard of you by the hearing of the ear, but now my eye sees you" (42:5).[2]

That transformational change—from having heard about God to experiencing God yourself—is what the wisdom of Jesus is most centrally about. In *Meeting Jesus Again for the First Time*, Marcus Borg writes the following:

The good news of Jesus' own message is that there is a way of being that moves beyond both secular and religious conventional wisdom. The path of transformation of which Jesus spoke leads from a life of requirements and measuring up (whether to culture or to God) to a life of relationship with God. It leads from a life of anxiety to a life of peace and trust. It leads from the bondage of self-preoccupation to the freedom of self-forgetfulness. It leads from life centered in culture to life centered in God.[3]

As those who are sent, it is only right that we seek to please God in all things and to grow up into the full stature of the sons and daughters of God, to use our God-given talents to develop ourselves and to be active collaborators in establishing God's reign of justice, peace, and right relationships. That transformation into the very experience of Jesus' intimacy with his Father is an "inside job," requiring our active cooperation, but carried forward by the Holy Spirit in mysterious ways that surpass our capacities. Our primary contribution is desire, and disposing ourselves through various practices and disciplines of the spiritual life so that the Potter finds the clay malleable and moist to work with.[4] The most important instrument in staying close to our heart's deepest desire is prayer.

"Ask…and Receive"

Our entire life, it seems, is a balancing act. In the beginning, as infants, it's the effort just to stand up on our feet. Then, it's to walk. After that, it's to ride a bike. A little later, we try balancing on skis or skates. Then it's a question of maintaining some sort of balance between our studies and social life. Once we become spiritually conscious adults, the challenge is still to find balance. A more theological way of putting it is that the challenge is to find our balance without falling into either of two heresies: Quietism—God can do it without me; and Pelagianism—I can do it without God.

Growing to mature discipleship means learning how to be both active and passive in our relationship with God. Prayer is active in the sense that we must do what only we can do from our side: to manifest desire. To want what God has to give. To ask for it, repeatedly. To open ourselves to receive it. God's gifts are not forced upon us. Look at the story where the risen Christ falls into step with two dejected disciples on the road to Emmaus on Easter Sunday and, unrecognized by them, interprets to them the things about himself in the scriptures to help them understand the events of the previous Friday. When they arrive at the village where the disciples were going, "Jesus walked ahead as if he were going on." Such is God's respect for our freedom. Obviously he came expressly to be with them and to help them, but they had to *ask* him to stay on with them and teach them more. And when "they urged him strongly, saying, 'Stay with us'…he went in to stay with them" and gave them an even greater revelation in the breaking of the bread as to just who it was that had been walking with them (Luke 24:28–32). This is the active side of prayer.

But prayer is also passive in the sense that purification and progress are the direct results of God's action upon us. Between Easter and Pentecost, the disciples *wait* patiently for the gift of the Holy Spirit to be given. There are, for example, ways of praying that are more active and ways that are more passive (at the end of this book I will provide some examples of and tools for both).

Important things take time to unfold, like the transformational shift from secondhand religion to firsthand religion. Things slowly ripen and develop within us. Consider Jesus' hidden years in Nazareth. As he matured into adulthood, it's not hard to imagine the local rabbi offering him a fast-track scholarship to the regional rabbinical school, or parents of marriageable daughters making discrete inquiries to Mary and Joseph about the interests of their very eligible and becoming bachelor son. He was obviously discerning his own call and letting it ripen within him before stepping forward to undertake his mission. And in the meantime, there were quiet years of inner listening.

The prayer life of a Christian must have a contemplative dimension. It must provide an area, a space of liberty, of silence, in which possibilities are allowed to surface and new choices—beyond routine choice—become manifest. It should create a new experience of time, a space that can enjoy its own potentialities and hopes. One's *own* time, but not dominated by one's own ego and its demands. It is a silent, solitary place within, where God is met and where the abundance of life becomes manifest.

The active life has a way of making us feel dependent on things. We need a ride here, a meal there, a loan or a subscription or a delivery. In the buying and selling of the marketplace, we are lured into dependency on the resources it offers, and we are conscripted into playing by its rules. They are the rules of scarcity. They tell us that what we need to survive and succeed is in short supply, so we had better shift into high gear or we will lose out. Prayer is the place where the claims of the world can fall away and be seen for what they are: illusions. And of all the illusions we must contend with, the illusion of scarcity is one of the most pernicious. The journey from illusion to truth is the heart of prayer.[5]

As one settles into a deep listening in passive prayer, the grasping ways of daily life seem comical. In that silence and solitude with God, how clear it seems that "letting go" is the only thing to do, since we cannot hang on anyway! In prayer, God's promise of abundance is revealed as present reality, all around us and within us, if only we will turn toward it and allow its expression in our living.

I got an impromptu lesson in how active and passive prayer work together by occasionally dropping in on a course in iconography at Unitas. An accomplished Romanian iconographer instructed people on the spirituality of writing icons, and then proceeded to the practical aspects. Participants first chose the image they wanted to paint. Then, under his guidance, they prepared the wood, traced the figure out on the wood, learned to mix the paint, and set to work. That, as I saw it, was active prayer: what we do from our side to prepare ourselves for what God wants to give.

When I stopped by at the end of the course for the blessing of the icons I was very impressed with the final results. One of the participants confided to me that the teacher had really done most of the work. They were able to apply some strokes of the brush, but he took a very active role and toward the end actually executed the finishing touches. That, to my eyes, was passive prayer. The whole process spoke of the way God works with us across the whole of our lives: We choose a pattern by which to live, and God actively works with us according to our desire.

Prayer, whether active or passive, helps us keep Ignatius's First Principle and Foundation front and center: "Your only desire should be this: to want and to choose what better leads to my deepening my life in you." In other words, it enables us to keep first things first. As C. S. Lewis commented, "All the beauty in nature withers when we try to make it an absolute. Put first things first and we get second things thrown in; put second things first, and we lose both first and second things."[6]

When first things are first, people may want for many material things, but they can still be happy. In visiting church-sponsored social work projects in the shantytowns surrounding large cities in certain countries of Africa and Latin America, I was always struck by the joyful faces of the children and the readiness of people to stop what they were doing and talk with us. In North America we have all the time-saving technology—our microwaves are humming and our Cuisinarts are whirring—but we don't have time to sit together as families to eat. We don't have time to stop and talk. In these settlements, people lived in dwellings with plywood walls, tin roofs, and earthen floors, but there was a sense that people were first, a sense of solidarity and belonging amongst those who lived there. When first things are first, you can live happily without many of the "second things" around which we build our lives. But when second things are put first, those who have them are restless and still searching for something or someone to fulfill the deepest desires of their hearts.

When first things are first, someone can interfere with our favorite television program, we can lose the game, sickness can prevent us from making a trip, a visitor can interrupt what we are working on, or we can find ourselves the object of unexpected criticism—and still be able to find peace and joy in life. There is great freedom in not being enslaved by what others think or what the weather does on game day or what we had on our list to get done today. This is what freedom from inordinate attachments looks like in practice. Freedom doesn't mean "no limitations" on me here and now. We are all limited by our historical situation, culture, our finances, our upbringing. While these influence us, they do not determine us. Within them we make our choices and retain our freedom. In our efforts to cultivate this inner state of being so vital to the spiritual life, we will do well to keep in mind some truths about the pattern of human growth.

The Pattern of Human Growth

In the evangelist Matthew's handling of the temptation story, it begins with the line, "Then Jesus was led by the Spirit into the wilderness to be tempted by the devil" (4:1).

Evil and temptation are part of our human situation. But the Spirit of God that is given to us enables us to grow in our struggle against them. Facing problems that arise as we do our best to live the two great commandments of loving God and others as ourselves is a way of becoming whole, holy, fully human, and spiritually free.

Problems should not, then, be seen as obstacles *in the way* of our vocations, but as *the way* in which we are called to embody Christ's sacrificial love for others. We may as well search for the pot of gold at the end of the rainbow as for a problem-free lifestyle. Since no way of life is without problems, the task is to discern *which set of challenges* is most worthy of our energy and holds the most promise for developing our capacity to love and serve as Jesus did.[7] The question is: Which way is the best way for me to serve?

The pattern of adult growth is not a straight line but a helix, an upwardly moving spiral in which we are constantly coming back and revisiting old issues. It is a process full of setbacks and frustrations. Accepting that growth is not linear and relinquishing the illusion of a smooth-flowing trajectory are necessary and will bring serenity to our striving for spiritual freedom. In his book *After the Ecstasy, the Laundry: How the Heart Grows Wise on the Spiritual Path*, Jack Kornfield writes:

The unfolding of the human heart is artful and mysterious. We might wish the path to enlightenment were orderly and predictable, but the ways of the heart are a landscape discoverable only in the journey. We cannot capture freedom and place it in time. For the mature spirit, freedom is the journey itself. It is like a labyrinth, a circle, a flower's petal-by-petal opening, or a deepening spiral, a dance around the still point, the center of all things. There are always changing cycles—ups and downs, openings and closings, awakenings to love and freedom, often followed by new and subtle entanglements. In the course of this great spiral, we return to where we started again and again, but each time with a fuller, more open heart....

When we compare a linear ascending path with a spiral unfolding, we find two quite different conceptions of spiritual fulfillment....The more circular vision of enlightenment presents freedom as a shift of identity. In this vision, too, we awaken to our true nature, and rest in a timeless freedom of spirit. We know that our true reality is beyond body and mind. And yet because we also live within this limited body and mind, the ordinary patterns of life may continue. In the prophets of Judaism, Christianity, and Islam, and among indigenous elders worldwide, awakened beings are more complex figures who combine sanctity and flawed humanity. The difference, though, is that the old difficulties are ungrasped, held in an easy and harmless manner.[8]

Maturity is the ability to live peacefully with limits. Maturity consists in making wise and loving choices. But learning how to love God and others in an integrated way comes only through daily practice. It is not through reading books but through trial and error in the laboratory of living that we discover how to fashion a dynamic and balanced life in which there is room for solitude and community, work and leisure, autonomy and intimacy, personal transformation and social reform, prayer and play. Finding the combination that will work for us is a highly personal matter. No one can give us a formula already worked out that only has to be applied. We must discover it for ourselves through personal experience.[9]

Whenever we lose our peace, we've lost sight of our creaturehood. Poverty of spirit and emotional chastity are not there. Poverty of spirit is recognition of my neediness, my dependence, my creaturehood. Emotional chastity is freedom from the addiction to feelings. When I lose my peace, it's because I have given in to some desolation in the realm of feelings; it might be the feeling of being overwhelmed, of being rejected, of not being loved, of fear. Freedom here does not mean elimination of my feelings, but awareness of them without enslavement to them. They're just there. What makes them good or bad is what I do with them.

That is where discernment enters in. If I'm going down a one-way street the wrong way and become aware of it, I turn off and turn around and get going in the right way. Discernment is recognizing I'm going the wrong way when such is the case. When the way I am responding to feelings is in blind reaction to them rather than out of a sense of choosing the most constructive way to respond to them, I am acting out of my addiction and am not demonstrating freedom. Discernment is a constant compass check: Am I going in the right direction?

In the Spiritual Exercises, Ignatius enunciates the principle of "acting against" the movement of feelings that are not taking us in the direction we want to go. "Acting against" is the pattern of growth. If I always go with the flow of my feelings, many of which will be coming from the false self and seeking comfort, honor, or control, I do not grow. In our fitness routines of jogging and swimming, for example, we act against the feeling to stay in bed longer in order to keep ourselves in good condition. If we never acted against those feelings of lethargy, we would lose our conditioning. Acting against creates a stance of freedom. It doesn't take the feelings away of how nice it would be to stay in bed—we recognize them, but just don't let them determine our behavior. "Okay, resistance. I understand that you're here. I'll even make space for you to be there. Stay as long as you need to, but right now I am choosing to act against what you are asking for."

The present moment in the movement for Christian unity calls for increased sharing of faith and life by people at the local level. But unless people occasionally make conscious decisions to "act against" their inclinations to stay with what they know and where they're comfortable, they will never cross over into their neighbor's place of worship and come to a positive appreciation of the gifts of devotional expression to be found there.

Many of the growthful experiences that people have—working in soup kitchens, serving in homeless shelters, becoming a Big Brother or Sister to a child, giving a month to building low-cost housing with Habitat for Humanity—only come about because they made a conscious decision to act against the false self's protective stance of "Oh, you don't need to do that." "Just stay at home where you'll be safe and secure." "Your money is growing nicely in your account; don't reduce it for that charity—let it accumulate."

The inner freedom represented in "acting against" explains why Dietrich Bonhoeffer returned to Germany and became an active participant in the anti-Nazi Confessing Church. It explains why Martin Luther King Jr. traveled to Birmingham, Alabama; why Christians witness to peace in danger zones of Latin America and the Middle East; why activists in our own day are willing to go to prison for their protests against national policies that menace our civilization with death and destruction; and it explains why Jesus went up to Jerusalem. "For freedom Christ has set us free," Paul proclaimed to the Galatians (5:1), adding ten verses later that this freedom had to be manifested in the love that calls us to serve one another.

Rededicating our lives daily to God means continually asking: "Where can I best use the gifts and resources I have been given? How can I make my time, my energy, my health, my material resources available for service in love?"

13

Falling Down and Getting Up Again

An ancient monastic was once asked by a young seeker, "What do you do in the monastery?" "Oh," he replied, "we fall down and we get up again. And we fall down and we get up again. And we fall down and we get up again." Life is about failing to meet standards and, as a result of each failure, growing in unimagined ways. We discover that we can fail in honesty and learn openness, that we can fail in chastity and learn love, that we can fail in greed and learn moderation, that we can fail in obedience and learn humility. The gospel leads us to ask what we are really intended to be: pursuers of the spiritual life or pursuers of perfection?[1] They are not one and the same, though they are both fueled by the hunger for God.

The Swiss psychiatrist Carl Jung believed that the human soul has an inborn need for God that is as powerful and urgent as the instinct for food and drink. This religious urge must be satisfied if we are to be psychologically healthy. When this fundamental function of the psyche is blocked, we create false gods and give ourselves over to them to the detriment of an authentic spiritual life. In her book *Addiction to Perfection*, Jungian analyst Marion Woodman suggests that striving for perfection is an attempt to meet this religious need, albeit through a counterfeit spirituality. Woodman sees the addiction to perfection as stemming from a cultural overemphasis on the masculine principle and suppression of the feminine. The masculine principle, symbolized by the head, values rationality, power, and perfection; the feminine, symbolized by the heart, cherishes feeling, relatedness, and mystery. The core spiritual issue in our culture today, according to Woodman, is "How do goal-oriented perfectionists find their way back to the lost relationship to their own heart?"[2]

In its own way, Christian preaching has contributed to the "disconnect" between head and heart. The biblical injunction to "be perfect as your heavenly Father is perfect" (Matt 5:48) has through the ages given Christians the impression that holiness consists in being completely successful or competent in overcoming all personal struggles and limitations or in being paragons of virtue. If to be true followers of Christ requires embodying the perfection of God, it is no wonder that the pursuit of perfection has often resulted in fear, hypocrisy, and legalism. Perfection, defined as errorlessness, is a human impossibility. Yet it has masqueraded for centuries as the nature of true Christian holiness.

In the verse "Be perfect, just as your heavenly Father is perfect" (Matt 5:48), the Greek word for perfect (*teleios*) has the sense of "completeness" or "full measure." It refers to the "wholeness of God," whose care and beneficence extends to all the peoples of the earth, regardless of their ability to respond to that divine love. Other translations better capture the correct nuance: "You must therefore set no bounds on your love, just as your heavenly Father sets none to his" (New Jerusalem Bible).

The context in which that biblical injunction appears supports this understanding. The "Be perfect" saying is immediately preceded by a description of God, who "makes the sun rise on the evil and the good" and who castigates those who love only people who love them. The real point of it is to imitate God's indiscriminate and inclusive love, to love without distinction. The passage does not advocate the pursuit of perfection as a striving for individual moral perfection; rather it advocates a lifelong stretching of one's capacity to love as God does.[3]

The identifying mark of a follower of Jesus is how they treat those who offend, sin against, or oppress them. By taking creative, nonviolent actions that confront the injustice and create space for reconciliation, a disciple of Jesus is identified as a child of God. We may genuinely feel that loving and forgiving and hoping for good things for people whom we can't stand is simply beyond our reach, impossible for us to do…alone. But we are not alone, unless we choose to be. We can reach far beyond our normal grasp if we ask for help.

Perfection for us human beings means that we are called to be humble vessels of Christ who recognize our tendency to miss the mark, who reject the ideal of excelling by personal strength, and who entrust ourselves totally to the power of grace.

When being a good Christian is seen as the perfect attainment of virtues, one's personal struggles and temptations must then be hidden from others and often even from oneself as well. Driven to do our best at school, on the job, in our relationships, we try to make ourselves into works of art. And we become more concerned with the servant than with those who need to be served. Working so hard to create our own perfection, we forget that we are called first of all to availability for service in love.

We would do better to think of ourselves as leaky buckets. Immersed in the ocean, they are always filled. We are better advised to accept the limits and imperfections the holes represent and stay immersed in the ocean of God's accepting, forgiving, unconditional love, than to try to become perfect by patching all our "holes."

When I officiated at Cecilia and Philippe's wedding, they were both rising stars in their professions. Philippe was a consultant with a large financial firm, and Cecilia was a marketing director at a children's educational software company. They had a baby daughter, Camille, eighteen months after they were married. And within eighteen months after that, twins! Cecilia shares her experience of "trying to be perfect" and recounts how, when she started accepting that her bucket was leaking, things took a big turn for the better.

> I am a strong, independent woman who prides myself on my capability to manage my own life. After the twins, I broke and felt that I could not do it anymore. I like to be in control, but with the twins I controlled nothing. It left me feeling helpless and depressed in addition to exhausted. I used to get bitter asking for help, because I wanted to do it on my own. I also felt that I was the one who could love my kids best. I was depressed at not being able to find the energy to read Camille, our oldest, a story at night. Depressed at not being able to hug the twins longer, to do what every mother gets to do when she has only one baby. I felt I was cheating my kids of the love I knew they deserved. I also left Philippe and myself aside. I had nothing left to give to anyone, my husband, friends, family and self. I would get angry with trying to plan activities because I was so tired.
>
> I realized that I was miserable doing it on my own, that I needed more people to help me make my life bearable.

In the middle of winter, I really let everything fall. I couldn't see straight, I couldn't even recognize what the real problem was. Now, with 20/20 hindsight, it is obvious to me: The problem was accepting the reality of the situation. This was simply the way it was with my family, my friends, my husband and myself—and the way it was going to be for some time to come.

Instead of feeling sorry for my exhausted and emotionally drained self, I said, "What can I do to change this?" That is when I started to ask for more help. And instead of feeling like I was letting myself down, I felt like I was making myself better. I was becoming me again and letting others love my kids to provide all the love that I wanted them to have. Believe me, it *does* take a village to raise a child.

My grandma says that "God never gives you more than you can handle." My addendum: and if God does, then God helps you find the support to manage. My mother, soon to be canonized into sainthood, spent three months with me this year, one on vacation and two as my support with the twins. My father moved us into our new house and came back when the twins were three weeks old to take on the 5 A.M. shift. My mother-in-law cooked meals for us for over half the year (during my bed rest and beyond birth) so that we wouldn't starve. And my father-in-law completely managed the maintenance, repairs, and painters to make our home livable. I give thanks to these people and tell them daily how much I appreciate their help.

Growth, real growth, the kind that changes us internally forever, comes slowly, and often through the hard, searing, humiliating, disappointing experience of failure. It's when we can no longer face ourselves, when we can go beyond guilt and shame to possibility, that we are ready to grow in new ways.

Cecilia's testimony reminds me of a story I heard in India of a water bearer who had two large pots. Each hung on opposite ends of a pole that he carried across his neck. One of the pots had a crack in it, and while the other pot was perfect and always delivered a full portion of water at the end of the long walk from the stream to the master's house, the cracked pot arrived only half full.

For two full years this went on daily, with the bearer delivering only one and a half pots of water to his master's house. Of course, the perfect pot was proud of its accomplishments, perfect to the end for which it was made. But the poor cracked pot was ashamed of its own imperfection, and miserable that it was able to accomplish only half of what it had been made to do.

After two years of what it perceived to be a bitter failure, it spoke to the water bearer one day by the stream. "I am ashamed of myself, and I want to apologize to you."

"Why are you ashamed?" asked the bearer. The cracked pot replied, "I have been able to carry only half my load for two years because this crack in my side causes water to leak out all the way back to your master's house. And because of my flaws, you have to do all this work and don't get full value from your efforts."

The water bearer replied, "As we return to the master's house, I want you to notice the beautiful flowers along the path." Indeed, as they went up the hill, the old cracked pot took notice of the sun warming the beautiful wildflowers on the side of the path, and this cheered it some. But at the end of the trail, it still felt bad because it had leaked out half the water, and so once again it apologized for its failure.

But the bearer said to the pot, "Did you notice that there were flowers only on your side of your path, but not on the other pot's side? I have always known about your flaw, and I took advantage of it. I planted flower seeds on your side of the path, and everyday while we walk back from the stream, you've watered them. For two years I have been able to pick these beautiful flowers to decorate my master's table. Without you being just the way you are, he would not have had this beauty to grace his house."

You might say we're all cracked pots, each of us with our own peculiar fissures. But in God's great economy, nothing goes to waste. When we acknowledge them and allow God to work through them, even our flaws contribute to the flowering of virtue in others along the way.

Free to Be Unfree

One of the aphorisms frequently repeated by John, my director and guide in the Spiritual Exercises, was "Free to be unfree." It is a prescription for the plague of perfectionism. It refers to how my "stuff" can come back on me at any time. Being free to be unfree means I can look at it without getting discouraged because I accept who I am as a mortal and sinner as well as a child of God. One day I go into the garden to weed and clean all the weeds out. Next week they're back again. Or, at the beginning of the planting season, I take a plow and turn up the rocks in my field and clean the field of them. Next year there are more rocks in the field. Being free to be unfree means accepting that work on my "stuff" is never finished; I can never put closure on it and say, "Well, I've dealt with that once and for all." Being free to be unfree means accepting that I am a work of God in process, that sometimes it's very messy, and that it is consistently a struggle. Christ conquered sin and death, but he didn't eliminate them from our experience. He invites us to come to full life the same way he did—by dying, not just at the end of our earthly existence, but dying daily to (letting go of, detaching from) the patterns of thinking and acting that do not lead to God. Every experience of new and fuller life comes to us through an experience of letting go, of dying. Like any process of new birth, it's messy! "Play in the mud," John would say. "Learn to be at home in the mud!"

You have to know in meditating on the mystery of the incarnation that not only are *our* "incarnations"—our lives—messy, but so was the son of God's! That is a valuable point of reference for the chaos, anxiety, fear of the unknown in our own lives. Imagine, if you will, the couple's journey from Nazareth to Bethlehem on through to the birth. The ride out of Nazareth toward the south is downhill. Anyone who has ever ridden a horse—even with a saddle on, much less a saddleless donkey— knows that riding downhill is not fun. You keep sliding up on the neck of the animal. It's uncomfortable, jerky, and difficult to maintain balance. For a woman nine months pregnant (airlines won't even admit a woman past six months pregnant on a one-hour flight today), it must have been *extremely* uncomfortable— and it was around a three-day journey. At nights, the soreness and added stress of sleeping poorly due to the conditions of roadside accommodations and the inability to find a comfortable position. Finally, arrival in the city of David, tired, dusty, sore, hungry, thirsty, feeling contractions and no accommodations available.

Imagine Joseph's frustration at being unable to provide for his wife, and anxiety over what to do.

A referral to a stable normally wouldn't excite, but in this situation any place is better than no place. Then comes the scramble to get Mary down onto something a little more comfortable than a donkey's back, to find water, a clean cloth, and all the while her contractions are becoming more severe. The sounds emanating from this young girl, who faces a whole new experience with nothing familiar around her to provide reassurance, sends Joseph's anxiety level and sense of inadequacy through the roof of the cave. And then the baby starts to come...something totally new for both of them. The intensity of delivery. The release of energy all around and the euphoric moment of holding a healthy child up in the air. Then the realization of things still to do: Clean the baby in those conditions, wipe the mother's forehead, take care of the afterbirth, get something around the child to keep it warm in the cool, damp night air, find a place to lay the infant down—oh, there's an animal's feeding trough...that'll do!

The event at Bethlehem reminds us that it was in the midst of circumstances such as these that saving grace came into the world. And it *continues* to come into the world in circumstances such as these! God seems to be drawn to "messy" and "raw," "simple" and "poor" much more than to "proper" and "clean," "elegant" and "rich." There is consolation in that for us all.

Going for Transformation

When I met Cheryl Broetje in Washington, D.C., at one of the Servant Leadership School weekends run by the Church of the Saviour, I realized I was talking with someone who had embraced the messiness of life, found God there, and learned to play in the mud. As I listened to her tell her story, it was clear that she had answered the call and dedicated her life to God each day in living out her response.

In December of 1982 my family took a "short-term missions trip" to Mexico to spend time with an organization by the name of Los Ninos. At that time Los Ninos gave direct relief to the impoverished families along the *frontera* area between Tijuana and Mexicali. Los Ninos enlisted volunteers like us, who would take soup to families living and working in the garbage dump on the west hills of Tijuana, or maybe glean leftover grapefruit and cabbage from the Imperial Valley to carry across to people squatting along ditch banks and dumps in Mexicali.

My husband and I had been working with junior high kids at our church. A hunger retreat we did with them sparked a desire to do something for those who were suffering. In the many experiences in Mexico through our relationship with Los Ninos over the years, there are a couple that stand out for me as signposts that pointed the direction ahead.

One day two of us were working with families on the hill west of Tijuana, a garbage dump with smoke rising everywhere. Families who live there do so in order to do their work of sifting through the garbage for tin and glass, which they then sell to in order to buy food. I will never forget looking from Tijuana, where you can see approximately fifteen miles on a clear day, into San Diego, California. On the other side of the border, you see white stucco houses with red tile roofs, the blue Pacific Ocean and sky. You see the beginnings of the green Imperial Valley, one of the richest agricultural areas in the world. As you stand there taking it all in, it occurs that this is like looking from hell into heaven.

The only thing keeping these people in hell that I could see at the time was a tall fence that we call "the border." I remember reading somewhere about that time a piece by Pope Paul VI in his 1969 "Instruction on the Pastoral Care of Migrants" that the right to work and feed the family precedes the right of a nation to establish borders and control exit and entrance to and from that nation. Since we are apple farmers who have worked side by side with Hispanic farmworker families for some thirty years now, this experience and the pope's message helped to galvanize our commitment to our people.

On that day we drove up the hill to a row of tiny mud-dung homes. Two of us went up to the door of one home just as the mother, Lupita, was coming out. She put a bowl of rice in our hands and told us to go in and feed her daughter. She was going next door, where a baby had just died. My friend and I went in the house to find not one, but two young adults tied loosely onto boxes, waiting for breakfast. We quickly discovered that neither of them had eyes at all; they couldn't hear and couldn't speak. (We were told later, that this was due in part to lack of vitamins and minerals in their diet.) As we sat down near the girl, my friend had the bowl of rice, so she began to feed her. I, wanting to be helpful but having nothing to offer, sat down by her side, with my arm on her shoulder.

Soon, she began to feel my face. After another bite or two, she gave me a hug; then, she just laid on me. A small encounter, but it changed my life radically. My friend and I both burst out in tears at that moment…and I immediately heard in my mind Matthew 25: "…as you have done it to the least of these, you have done it to me." I realized that this poor, blind, deaf young Mexican woman became Jesus for me that day.

When we left, I knew that my understanding of "missions" had forever changed. It wasn't about good, white, wealthy, Christian me going to help poor, brown, dumb her…it was about two people letting love draw them together in a mutually beneficial way, and both the stronger for it. I had no idea that this would be the seed that would grow into an organization that I would found later on. I only knew that we had to find ways to get others to come and see what we had seen and experienced.

So, we did exactly that. One day, while on the way to visit a mother of nine in a garbage-dump home in Mexicali, our driver stopped to talk to three little boys alongside the road. He apparently knew them, and asked why they were not in school. They told him that they didn't have any water to wash their clothes, and they couldn't go to school until their uniforms were clean. Later, while visiting with their mother, a water truck pulled alongside the house and filled three fifty-gallon water barrels. When I asked how that happened, I was told that the mother had made fifty braided friendship bracelets and sold them that morning to Los Ninos staff in order to buy water. I knew that those boys would be able to go to school the next day.

That experience filled me with an incredible desire to help. So, we began to buy up bracelets, blouses, towels from around that area, to sell in our church office. Before long, we were regularly selling Mexican handicrafts. We also organized a walk-a-thon that became a yearly event for five or six years, to help build and strengthen schools in these areas. When we eventually bought a building for The Center For Sharing to move into, one of the programs we housed was an imports craft shop.

My life has evolved greatly since 1982. The Center For Sharing (whose mission statement became "calling forth the gifts of all persons through Christ-centered community") has engaged individuals and given birth to approximately fifteen service programs over the years so far. When we took small groups around the world on other "trips of perspective," we began to see that all our service efforts to relieve poverty and its life-killing effects were just a drop in the ocean. What was really needed was to raise up more servants and leaders in a culture that has been utterly seduced by money and self-serving agendas.

In 1995 we were introduced to those who were working with a "Servant Leadership School" associated with Church of the Saviour in Washington, D.C. Over the years I had read every book of Elizabeth O'Connor's that I could find[4] and greatly admired their sold-out approach to serving Christ, the world, and one another. *Sojourners* magazine had been an important link between my own religious questions and frustrations with the institutional church, and those who were out there somewhere trying to practice their spirituality. The majority of them were laypeople just like me. These books, mentors, and friends gave me the courage to do the same, with little clue about where I was going, but a growing belief that with God all things were possible. The important thing was to do something!

Since 1995 we have offered five nine-month servant leadership courses in Washington State as well as ongoing à la carte classes wherever people will have us.[5] These courses are designed to evoke passion for God and the desire to become partners with God and others, in the work of restoring God's dream for the world in some specific way, among a specific group of people. We have affectionately been referred to as "dream brokers." This is both thrilling work and very difficult, marginal (because it's seen as radical) work. We are going for transformation, not social service management. That means our continuing transformation as well as that of those we serve.

To daily rededicate ourselves to God is to answer one's call, to accept being sent, and to "go for transformation" amidst all the messiness of daily living and the complex web of relationships in which we find ourselves.

14
Keeping Your Intention Sharp

The biographies of inspiring people yield valuable insights for our own living. When Nelson Mandela went to prison he was forty-four years old. When he came out in his surprising release from a life sentence he was seventy-one. How did he maintain his motivation and keep his spirit resilient and strong over twenty-seven years of incarceration? In the early years of his imprisonment, he was routinely charged with the smallest infractions, like being sentenced to isolation for failing to stand when a guard walked into the room. In isolation one was deprived of company, exercise, and even food; one received only rice water three times a day.

> I have found that one can bear the unbearable if one can keep one's spirit strong even when one's body is being tested. Strong convictions are the secret of surviving deprivation; your spirit can be full even when your stomach is empty....To survive in prison, one must develop ways to take satisfaction in one's daily life. One can feel fulfilled by washing one's clothes so that they are particularly clean, by sweeping a hallway so that it is empty of dust, by organizing one's cell to conserve as much space as possible.[1]

Although there are more stirring passages in Mandela's autobiography, I keep returning to lines like these. Their simple witness speaks so effectively of the power in faithful attentiveness to quotidian realities. Through twenty-seven years, Mandela stayed close to his ideals and his desire for the people of Africa. It kept his spirit resilient and strong.

> During my lifetime I have dedicated myself to this struggle of the African people....I have cherished the ideal of a democratic and free society in which all persons live together in harmony and with equal opportunities. It is an ideal which I hope to live for and to achieve. But if needs be, it is an ideal for which I am prepared to die.[2]

I look for inspiration in movies, too. In the opening scene of the film *Cast Away*, Chuck Nolan (played by Tom Hanks) is in Moscow pointing to a giant digital wall clock and screaming at new FedEx Russian employees about the importance of time and efficiency. He flies back to the United States just in time for a Christmas dinner with his girlfriend Kelly and other friends, but in the middle of it his pager goes off and he has to leave again. "We'll have to open Christmas gifts in the car on the way to the airport," he says to Kelly.

Cast Away holds the mirror up to those of us who, in becoming adults, have been conditioned to believe that efficiency is more important than love. We have difficulty in taking time to just *be with*. We think we must get on with more important things.

When Chuck's plane crashes in the Pacific Ocean and he finds himself marooned on an island, the only remnant of his former life that survives with him is the heirloom pocket watch Kelly had given him at the airport with her picture in it. He sets it up in his cave. Her picture gives him a reason to live. As we watch him put to ingenious use the contents of the FedEx boxes washing up on shore, we get an important new perspective. The company motto on the boxes—"The world on time"—now makes Chuck laugh.

He has come to see that love is the "why" of life: why we are functioning at all, what we want to be efficient *for*. Love is the fundamental energy of the human spirit, the fuel on which we run, the wellspring of our vitality. In contrast, efficiency is the "how" of life. It relates to how we handle the demands of daily living, how we survive, grow, and create, how we deal with stress, how effective we are in our functional roles and activities.[3]

There is no question for the Apostle Paul in chapter 13 of his Letter to the Corinthians what comes first. Love should be the beginning of and reason for everything. Efficiency relates to "how" love expresses itself. Toward the end of the film, when Chuck says to Kelly, "I never should have gotten on that plane. I never should have gotten out of the car," he recognized how our concerns about efficiency can eclipse the love they are meant to serve.

The problem is not whether we want love *or* efficiency; it is which we want *more*. To which do we give the higher priority? On the surface it seems natural to value love more highly. Religion, philosophy, art, give it lip service, but it is very difficult to put this priority into practice. No matter how noble our words about love may sound, we are conditioned to believe efficiency is everything. It is the standard by which every person and enterprise is judged in our modern, developed culture. We weigh people's worth by how well they function.[4]

What is worse, our society encourages us to believe that love is just another function, an ability to be learned and refined.

There are techniques for love, we are told, and if we use them well, we will have something to show for it: well-managed, smoothly functioning relationships, social popularity, emotional security, sexual fulfillment. Seen from this perspective, expressions of love become commodities, loved ones become objects, and the pains of love become problems to be solved. In other words, love itself ends up being measured by the yardstick of efficiency. By submitting all else to the gods of efficiency and achievement, the human race has achieved the highest level of efficiency in history. But it is clear that our love has not kept up with our efficiency. Our technology has made us more destructive to one another and our planet. Whether at the macro or micro level, our tendency is to sacrifice love for "progress."[5]

If we were to do a modern rewrite of Paul's great hymn to love, it might sound something like this: "If I have a cell phone, a laptop, a palm pilot, but do not have love, I am a noisy CD player or a pulsating car alarm. If I have all knowledge and a perfect 4.0, but do not have love, I fail. Or if I understand the mysteries of the stock market, but do not have love, I gain nothing." A modern version of the gospel would likely contain the gloss: "There are *four* things that abide: efficiency, faith, hope, and love. But the greatest of these is love."

Paul would have us grasp that there is nothing more beautiful and freeing than living with conscious dedication to love. The way of love invites us to become vessels of love. It asks for vulnerability rather than self-protection. But the invitation of love is as challenging as it is beautiful. Saying "yes" to the invitation to love will hurt you. It will upset your stability. It will put your security at risk. Saying "yes" to love engages you in an immense internal warfare, not only with your fear of being hurt, but also with the efficiency-worship of the world that displaces love as the top priority.

As those who are called by Love and sent to bring love, our constant task must be to claim love as a treasure. Our faith tells us that we are created by love, to live in love, for the sake of love. It tells us that love is the ground of our being. In the words of the thirteenth-century Sufi poet Ramon Lull:

> They asked the Lover, "Where do you come from?"
> He answered, "From love."
> "To whom do you belong?"
> "I belong to love."
> "Who gave you birth?"
> "Love."
> "Where were you born?"
> "In love."
> "Who brought you up?"
> "Love."
> "How do you live?"
> "By love."
> "What is your name?"
> "Love."
> "Where do you come from?"
> "From love."
> "Where are you going?"
> "To love."
> "Where do you live?'
> "In love."[6]

There lies the challenge! To live in love. To live according to that priority in the moment-to-moment experiences of our lives. To be consciously, energetically alive and involved *in* love. Infinite possibilities of action spring forth from being alive-in-love, and it is a much more frequent occurrence than we tend to think.

Love pervades our existence in an endless procession of actions, thoughts, and feelings. It is present in all feelings of caring and of connectedness. We think of falling in love as a rare occurrence, but it is the most ordinary of human events; we do it all the time. We fall in love whenever we give ourselves to someone or something. We have fallen in love with everything and everyone we hold dear. It is a special experience, because it wakes us up. It thrills us and hurts us and makes us conscious of being alive. We would like to experience the joy and energy of love without being vulnerable to its pain, but there is no way to do that. To love is to care, to care is to give ourselves, and giving ourselves means becoming vulnerable. When we "fall" in love, we in effect fall from our sense of control and separateness, from whatever towers of false security we have constructed for ourselves. We fall into wonder and wakefulness, joy and agony.[7]

Intentionality

When we are really dedicated to living in love and to acting from love, really dedicated to the "why" of life, the "hows" begin to flow. Life goes on, struggles continue, but saying yes to love gives us a vision of what our problems are for, why our struggles have value beyond efficiency. In *Cast Away*, just before pushing off from the island in his raft, Chuck scraped a message on the rock in case he died at sea: "Chuck Nolan was here 1500 days. Escaped to sea. Tell Kelly Frears, Memphis, TN, I love you."

In saying yes again and again to love, we get a glimpse of what life is really all about. Those we love are significant and precious—not just for the choices they make or the actions they take, but for their very presence. We are so busy, so occupied with many little things, that we become blind to the preciousness of their presence. We need to hear it again, even in the modern version: there is efficiency, faith, hope, and love, but the greatest of these is love.

Love continues to beckon to us, hoping to catch us with an open heart. The way toward love is intention. It is the most essential, the most completely *human* thing about us. It is a stretch of the will, reaching out and opening toward that which we desire. We cannot truly say yes to love alone. Grace makes it possible and brings it to fruition. We can neither earn it nor make it happen. But grace invites our participation. What we contribute is awareness. We cannot be intentional if we are asleep. When our intention is to live in love and to act from love, we consciously accept to receive and respond to a gift. If the "why" of life is love, and the "how" is efficiency, then the "who" is God.[8] God is the giver of the gift, and we the responder. Remember Ignatius's First Principle and Foundation: "Your one and only desire should be this: to want and to choose what better leads to my deepening my life in you."

How can we dedicate ourselves, consecrate ourselves, open ourselves to love? We open ourselves by becoming aware of God's presence and involvement in our lives. God *is* love, and is the Source of all the love in our lives. When we become aware of the presence of God, albeit in a flash, and say yes to it, that *is* our consecration to love, our conscious participation in it. The more frequent the awareness, the more constant the consecration. A continually renewed immediacy of the Divine touch is at the heart of living our consecration to love. How does one do that?

The normal approach would be to make lots of promises and resolutions. But resolutions tend to be "I" centered and rooted in the false-self ego. When I try to find security in resolutions, it is something ego thinks it is going to carry through on and accomplish all by itself. A resolution flows from voluntarism, willpower. But we don't know what is going to happen in the future, so is it wise to gear ourselves up to ride roughshod over any variety of circumstances that might present itself?

Better we should commit to constant cultivation of our deep desire. All we can do is stay humbly and simply close to our deepest desire in hope.

> You have heard that it was said to those of ancient times, "You shall not swear falsely, but carry out the vows that you have made to the Lord." But I say to you, do not swear at all, either by heaven...or by the earth...or by Jerusalem.... And do not swear by your head, for you cannot make one hair white or black. Let your word be "Yes" or "No"; anything more than this comes from the evil one. (Matt 5:33–37)

Anything more than just staying close to my deepest desire and saying yes or no as things happen and choices present themselves is suspect.

This does not negate the import of vows and promises that married people, religious, and consecrated laity make. What it underlines is that we have to renew the intention of that promise every day to keep it alive and warm and authentic. At a particular moment in time, I might dedicate my life or this work to God. But for all that, it is not "done." If I do not rededicate myself or my engagement in a particular work each day, I should not be surprised if one day I wake up and experience the promise I made as a restriction, a burden, and don't want to live consistently with it anymore. The power in this is that when I do *not* place my security in the simple fact that a promise was made, I am obliged to stay much more connected to the content of that promise in order to keep it alive and active.

A religious community had a particular personnel need, and one of the members said to the superior: "I'll go if you need me." To which the superior responded: "That's not good enough. You have to *choose* to go. Without that, when things get difficult, you'll only complain." It is our intentionality, kept alive and active through frequent rededication, which keeps us faithfully engaged in hard times as well as good times.

Be Guided by Your Deepest Desire

I confess that my tendency is to want to get something all sorted out and fenced in with resolutions and then to live secure within that little closure. But the fact is: I don't know what is going to happen. The most real and authentic thing for me to do is simply to stay in close contact with my deepest desire and to be guided by that in any decisions that present themselves.

This requires two kinds of courage. First, we must be open to things as they are, and resist from projecting our expectations onto reality. Second, we must be willing to respond from our deepest desire, no matter how impractical or risky it may be.[9]

The Bible offers us both positive and negative role models. In this case, it tells a story of a man, Jonah, who exhibited neither kind of courage: He both projected his expectations onto reality and failed to act from his deepest desire.

God put out a call to Jonah. God had a mission on which to send him: to warn Nineveh of its coming punishment. But Jonah didn't choose to deliver that message. He first slipped out of town and bought a cruise ticket thinking that he could escape God's presence on the high seas. Even after being thrown overboard and spending three days in the belly of a great fish and being belched up on the beach, he could not muster the desire to deliver God's message to the Ninevites when asked a second time. He did it, but he didn't *want to*.

It is likely that Jonah hated the Ninevites because of the military threat they posed to the northern kingdom of Israel. It is easy to imagine that an Israelite would welcome God's judgment of Nineveh and project the expectation that God would seize any pretext to destroy it since it threatened the people of Israel. Jonah would not have gotten in the way of such a gratifying event. Jonah did not want to warn his enemies of God's coming judgment. He was afraid they might heed his message and actually repent. And he knew that if they did, God would be merciful and pardon them. He didn't want that to happen. And sure enough, the Ninevites responded with edifying rapidity to the warning that Jonah eventually was pressured into giving them. Nineveh had forty days to repent, but needed only one. As soon as the people were warned, they turned to God. All of them, even the animals, abstained from food and water as a sign of sorrow for their sins. Jonah, as you might expect, was miserable and angry. He had gone through the motion of bringing God's word to them; he had observed the letter of God's instruction to him but not the spirit. His heart wasn't in it. There was no intentionality. Jonah did not *want* the Ninevites to hear and respond to God's warning. Jonah wasn't dedicated to bringing that word of God to the Ninevites at all. He just did it because he felt trapped and didn't know where else to go to escape.

How many with vows or promises made are in that place right now: I don't want to be here, doing this, but I don't know how to get out of it? When those vows were made, the dedication they represented to God or to a spouse or both was alive and active. Somewhere along the way the fire went out because one (or one's partner, or both) stopped affirming, saying "I love you," doing considerate things, tending the fire consciously and actively, and lost the intentionality in the process. The Bible is full of stories of people like Solomon, David, Peter, who received special calls and special graces but who at some point along the way lost their intentionality and went to sleep. If it can happen to the best of us, it can happen to the rest of us!

Renewing Our Consecration Daily

How can we dedicate ourselves, consecrate ourselves, to the Source of love? The word "consecration" comes from the Latin root *com* (with) and sacer (sacred). It implies intentionally participating with the divine, consciously participating in love, intentionally opening ourselves to accept the divinely given gift.[10]

To claim my desire for love most fully, I must feel that desire, right here and now in the midst of my daily activities. To say yes to love, I need to form my intention with authentic presence in this real moment. To consecrate my intention, I must consciously be involved with God—realize that God is involved with all of us, right here, right now. This can happen fully only with present-centered awareness. A French Jesuit priest of the early eighteenth century, Jean Pierre de Caussade, gave us the phrase "the sacrament of the present moment." In a sacrament we are aware that God is present to strengthen, to heal, to renew.

Brother Lawrence of the Resurrection, a sixteenth-century Carmelite, speaks in the classic entitled *The Practice of the Presence of God*,[11] of cultivating the sense of God's presence. He tells us how he does it with "a little interior glance," a simple recognition of divine presence. It can be more a feeling than a thought. It does not necessarily mean looking inward; it simply *happens* interiorly. It is a contemplative look Godward. It is an attitude of the heart leaning toward the truth of God's presence, or a flash of the mind opening to the remembrance of being in love. Little interior glances are simple movements of the heart, unadorned remembrances happening within the ordinary activities of our daily lives.

There are times when we are caught up in activity or difficulties, and we feel distant from both God and our own desire for love. In such moments we can only claim our desire to desire. And because that is what is real in that moment, it is sufficient. Every attempt we make is an expression of our desire to open to love and to let love flow through us. It may not feel like enough;

sometimes it feels like nothing. But it is sufficient because it is real.

The sanctity of consecration comes from grace empowering our intention to be as involved as we most authentically can be. With time and repeated effort, our consecration becomes as ordinary and natural as breathing, until every act of every day is simply sacred, until each moment is infused with love and presence. Authentic spiritual practice is consecration in action. It is feeling our deepest desire, claiming it as freshly born hope, offering it to God, and consciously living it as fully as we can.[12]

There are things we can do to encourage ourselves to remember our desire to live in love, to live from love. When you have something important to remember, how do you normally try to keep it in mind? Whatever has helped remind you of other things can also help remind you of God's presence. Gerald May offers a variety of ideas in his book *The Awakened Heart*:

- Try switching your watch to your other wrist, or your ring to your other finger, taking an interior glance every time you notice the difference.
- Set your digital watch to beep on the hour as a reminder.
- Leave little notes or symbols where you will encounter them: in your calendar or on your mirror, on your desk, on the steering wheel of your car. These might be little memos like "remember." You will devise your own code words or objects.
- Look for the divine presence in other people's eyes, or let the faces of people on the street be little homecomings.
- Tag special places, objects, and sounds with reminding significance. If there are certain things in your house or office,

or places that you regularly pass while walking or driving your car, dedicate them: for example, "I hope to remember love's presence every time I pass this picture or plant, or whenever I hear the phone or a doorbell ring, or pass that advertisement on the road."

- Program your computer to put a message box on your screen at intervals throughout the day with an invitation to look within.

- Gather with those few people in your life who truly support your desire. It is a powerful reminder to simply be in the presence of such friends.

- Look at your formal religious participation. Worship services are in part intended to help you remember what is most important in your life. Do they do that for you? Are there ways you can help make them better reminders?[13]

As May notes, these practices are not ends in themselves. They are merely ways of helping us deepen a basic attitude that we can then bring into the rest of our life and activities. In the midst of all these situations, a little interior glance is like an exchange of smiles across the room at a party with someone you love, or like a quick eye contact that refreshes your conscious connection with each other. At the end of the day, a good daily reflection question is: At what times was I most absent today, most kidnapped by some activity, most closed off? As you identify such times, carefully consider how the forgetfulness happens and what, if anything, you might do about it.[14]

The author of the fourteenth-century classic on contemplative prayer, *The Cloud of Unknowing*, made this provocative assertion: "I tell you this: one loving blind desire for God alone is more valuable in itself, more pleasing to God and to the saints, more beneficial to your own growth, and more helpful to your friends, both living and dead, than anything else you could do." How could this be so? My single desire for God will be of more help to others because my single desire will give birth to the kind of action that will really help them. It is not a question of desiring God instead of doing helpful actions, but *desiring God as the source of the actions that are going to be really helpful.* It is that simple. Put efficiency first, and the world gets to be the way it is today. Put love first, and the whole meaning of efficiency is transformed.[15]

The Only Agenda Is...

It's one thing to read reflections like the above and another to find them incarnated in the life of someone you know. Debra is a wife and mother of two. I knew her when she danced before the Lord in worship at the Ohio State University Newman Center in Columbus, before she went on to be a campus minister herself at Loyola in Chicago, married, and began raising a family with her husband, Greg. For years she experienced strange occurrences in her body until one day it all came clear.

My body seemed to be an enigma until three years ago when these mysterious symptoms finally let themselves be known by a name, multiple sclerosis. Then, a grieving process had its way with my mind and heart and soul.

Everything that I had known or thought about up until this time was somehow different. Everything was now up for grabs: now what? What about my husband and children? I had come to midlife ill-equipped for this situation. I'd prided myself on becoming an independent woman, and here I was looking at a disease that could take any or all parts of my body—even my mind. I had no place or time for this in the plan for my life.

The chronic, debilitating effects of MS, coupled with the powerlessness of modern medical science in the face of this mystery, invited me to look at the options. I could take the antidepressant and buoy my emotions for awhile, but I knew deep inside there was a spiritual walk I needed to take. I was terrified, but needed to face the truth about who I am and who is the God that I thought I knew since I was a child. I didn't like this place. And for awhile, I threw myself a huge self-pity party. I cried a lot, and cried more when I encountered the insensitivity of those who have no idea how lonely and terrifying this place can get. I wanted to be normal and healthy like them, too.

Yet, as I cried (and kicked and screamed) and lived with the painful reality that MS was a part of my life, I knew that I could only venture on this journey alone. I didn't know anyone who was or had been living in this place of my mind and heart. I didn't even know in all of my theological and spiritual readings where to find a guide or companion, save for the last days of Jesus' life—there was someone who knew the devastation of defeat and humiliation. And then he died and was into the whole resurrection scene…what about the unglamorous reality of going forward with the defeat and humiliation? There was no roadmap and the territory was completely unfamiliar; it felt as I though I didn't even know the God I thought I loved. And God, whoever that was now, seemed strangely distant and silent. There was no relief from the pain and the devastation of these dark and lonely days. For months, in an attempt to pray, I uttered only one word: "mercy."

I clung to passages in scripture that said the Holy Spirit knew our groanings and just hoped against the despair I felt that somewhere, somehow, Someone was listening. I didn't even know how to name this awful place, except to think that this must be what the mystics named "the dark night of the soul." To be adrift and feel so cut off from everything, with no answers to comfort.

The one constant was the love of a few close friends and my family—my husband still expected me to be Debbie, and my children still wanted their mother to be Mom. They still teased and laughed and expected me to laugh with them, too. They waited as I explored the depths of my heart and soul...alone. I didn't want to be a burden to my loves, yet I could easily become a victim of this disease. Together, we journey through life aware of the fact that life is hard. This awareness opens our hearts to compassion and the greater power of love. There are daily obstacles in living with chronic illness that requires us to be more honest and direct with one another...passionately investing in a commitment where love is the verb. I am so thankful for their love and commitment to helping me live with and move beyond the limitations of this disease...inviting me to laugh especially at myself.

Somewhere in this time of letting go of my own expectation and dreams, a new place was unfolding in my spirit.

I began to appreciate that all of life is gift. That every breath, every sight, every sound, every person is a gift of God's handiwork. There is no agenda other than that of loving. Living with MS teaches me that I must love myself and others as God loves us. That we are all connected at all times even when we're not feeling connected. That the others who suffer with the same disease or any other illness or struggle are all my brothers and sisters. That the researchers who devote their life's work to finding a cure for us are my brothers and sisters. That every time I offer my body for the sake of research so that someday, others may be spared this disease, I am giving a gift to others. That there really are no labels like "MS" or "cancer" or "normal." There are just people who were created by the same God who made us and who asked that we walk humbly with our God and one another. I used to think it was independence I sought. Now, I recognize the necessity of interdependence—how God made us all to live together in love and peace and joy.

Slowly, like hints of spring come gingerly through the winter cold, I began to see glimmers of a new place I'd not known before. I sensed a presence, a benevolent, gracious presence, near me and all around me as I saw the sun set, or heard the voice of Andrea Bocelli singing a prayer, or the compassionate eyes of someone who sensed my pain and struggle, saying, "I'm praying for you." Sweet balm to an aching spirit. And…one sign—the colors of the rainbow—has consistently been a sign for me of God's nearness.

An old dream that I had put on the "someday" shelf came due. "Someday" became "today." With the encouragement of my artist friend, Alice, I began to paint with watercolors, to feast my eyes and hands and heal my heart through the joy of creating with color. My experience found poetic expression in these words from the novel *The Sparrow* by Mary Russell, paraphrasing the poet Aeschylus: "In our sleep, pain which cannot forget falls drop by drop upon the heart, until, in our own despair, against our will, comes wisdom through the awful grace of God."

Somehow, through the tears of hopelessness and anger, I began to understand that God had never been far from me. God's awful grace was showing me that I had gotten my facts confused. Yet, once the truth was faced and the shattered illusions grieved, I knew I had missed seeing something important: I thought the plan for my life was my doing. It never was. It never will be. It was never about how good I was or how much I could accomplish with my life. It had always been about how good God is and what a wondrous plan God has to prosper me.

All I need to do is to make the choice for love. No matter what limitations my body lived—even with legs that no longer worked—I could still dance my life. MS could rob me of some of life's joys and pleasures, but it would not take away my choice for life. I realized that I had taken so much for granted for most of my life—like walking and talking and seeing and thinking. I used to cry over silly things; now I'd much rather be laughing. MS has been my wake-up call and continues to be my daily challenge. Ever since I was a child, I was drawn to the stories with the happy endings. We are called through Good Friday's devastating storms and death to the Easter rainbow.

Each day, whenever I choose to love, to let go of my agenda and let God's agenda take over, I am no longer disabled. I am a new creation of love's energy abounding.

These words from Thoreau's *Walden Pond* speak to my heart: "We must learn to reawaken and keep ourselves awake, not by mechanical aids, but by an infinite expectation of the dawn, which does not forsake us in our soundest sleep. I know of no more encouraging fact than the unquestionable ability of man to elevate his life by conscious endeavor. It is something to be able to paint a particular picture, or to carve a statue, and so to make a few objects beautiful. But it is far more glorious to carve and paint the very atmosphere and medium through which we look….To affect the quality of the day—that is the highest of the arts."

All our themes are there in Debra's story: Know who you are. Live your calling to the full. Let go of results. Daily rededicate your life to God. And most particularly from this chapter: falling down and getting up again; playing in the mud; keeping your intention sharp; consecrating yourself to love. Some of her statements fly like banners in the wind:

"There is no agenda other than that of loving."

"All I need to do is to make the choice to love."

"Each day, whenever I choose to love, to let go of my agenda and let God's abundance take over, I am no longer disabled. I am a new creation of God's energy abounding."

Spiritual freedom is not a "thing" that can be hung onto; rather, it is an inner condition of the spirit which, like a garden, can be continually cultivated no matter what your physical condition is.

15
Freedom Tools

If spiritual freedom is not a "thing" that can be hung onto, but rather an inner garden of the spirit that must be continually cultivated with use of the right tools, what are some of those tools?

We have seen how the Spiritual Exercises of St. Ignatius are really about developing a discerning heart and providing people with tools for discernment in their decision making (discussed in Step Two) as they head back into mission with Christ. A general, all-seasons tool like this is necessary because the only constant in life is change, and life will continually present us with decisions that need to be made. The challenge is to stay close to the deep desire to find, love, and serve God in all things and to keep the intentionality alive "to see thee more clearly, love thee more dearly, follow thee more nearly, day by day."

At the end of the Step Two, I related how affected I was by the recurring critique of Christianity that I encountered from Westerners in India: "Christianity doesn't teach us practical methods by which we can go deeper in the spiritual life." I want to end this book with three very practical ways of daily dedicating one's life to God, of keeping one's intentionality alive and active, of moving toward spiritual freedom.

Earlier in our reflections on Step Four, I wrote about both active and passive methods of prayer each having a place in our spiritual lives. The first and third ways described here are active and the second one is passive. The first one is the primary tool for staying close to our desire to find, love, and serve God in all things and to keep that intentionality fresh.

A. The Examen

The examen[1] is a way for us to literally submit our lives to God each day. In addition, it is a very effective instrument for helping us become aware of God acting in our lives throughout the day. It sharpens our awareness of where and how God is acting. This addresses one of the key obstacles to our desire to grow spiritually: We are not in the habit of *looking*. We all need to develop a discerning attitude in which we are seeking God in all things and keeping that intention close to our hearts.

In the examen, we bring the personal encounters, the events, and the feelings of the day before the Lord so he can enlighten us as to their meaning and significance and gradually change our way of seeing into his own faith vision. His faith vision is the way he looked at the world during his lifetime. He could see the world as it was and at the same time see the reign of God that was coming into the world through him and taking root in people's hearts.

Everything, then, is data for discernment as we learn to look at our lives with a faith vision. The faith vision enables us not just to see the event or encounter the feelings around it, but to see what God is doing there. The conversation you had with a friend over lunch. The feelings about your job that emerged in the course of the staff meeting. The unexpected letter that came in the mail. The article that seemed to leap out as you were reading the newspaper this morning. The examen brings all these things and the feelings you have about them into the presence of

Christ, asking him to enlighten you on their true meaning. This practice effectively develops within us a discerning heart ready to follow the Spirit's lead.

If one uses Teresa of Avila's three key ingredients for the spiritual life—self-knowledge, rootedness in Christ, and perseverance—as a measuring stick for the value of any particular practice, the daily examen of consciousness rises to the top. Through it, one grows daily in self-knowledge. And because the particular focus of the examen has been arrived at in dialogue with Christ and through his choosing, one remains reliant on him throughout in striving to improve in the area he has indicated. Finally, because one's strength and hope is drawn from him and not from oneself and one's own resources, perseverance is made possible. No wonder then that Ignatius indicated to his followers to stick with this practice even if they had time for nothing else. It is a powerful instrument. In striving to know ourselves better, it is important that we become aware of the motivations for why we do things. This is precisely what the Lord reveals to us during the time of the examen. One of its fruits is a peace that comes from living in alignment with the Holy Spirit's lead in our lives.

In practice, the examen is very simple. The whole process takes from five to ten minutes. There are four steps.

Step 1: An Act of Presence

Imagine yourself in the presence of Jesus. Express the hope that with his help you can understand the deeper significance of what seemed like just another ordinary day (or a very special or traumatic day). It is a mental *dialogue*, not an introspective monologue. Ask to understand the events of your day as an integral part of your unique spiritual journey to God.

Step 2: A Petition for Light, Wisdom, and Humility

Ask for light that you may see clearly what the Lord wants you to see. Ask for wisdom that you may understand what he shows you. Ask for humility that you may accept it and learn from it.

Step 3: Examination with Thanksgiving and/or Sorrow

Now let the day prayerfully pass by in stream of consciousness like a moving train. You are watching it go by with Jesus. Let him take the lead in stopping the train whenever he wants to look at something more closely. When Jesus stops the flow by bringing something to your attention, look carefully at the feelings you have around it. Whenever you feel comfortable in his presence in looking at some event in your day, say a simple "Thank you." Whenever you feel uncomfortable and know he is displeased, say "I'm sorry," and ask him why he is displeased. His answer turns what seems like an obstacle into an opportunity for spiritual growth. Everything is potentially a gift if we can see how it is either taking us to God or obstructing our way.

As we become attuned to see things as he sees them, we may uncover both false joy and false guilt. Suppose, for example, that you feel very good about something that you did during the course of the day, but not when you look at it during the examen. As you look at it through Jesus' eyes, you see that you were seeking your own self-advancement and not the advancement of his reign in people's hearts. Or suppose that you got angry with someone. Afterward, you felt guilty about it, but in looking at it through Jesus' eyes at the time of the examen, you see that he is not displeased. He shows you that your anger was justified and appropriate. And so it goes: We can grow in self-knowledge.

Step 4: Request Help for Tomorrow

Resolutions often don't work because they are "I" centered; they are built on our own sense of self-will—"I can do it if I just try hard enough." We fail because our resources are limited. The examen invites one to keep Christ and his resources at the center of focus. In looking at what is ahead the next day, we do so with the awareness that we are reliant on him to give fruit to our efforts.

There is a way to make daily use of the examen particularly effective, to tighten the screws on it, as it were. Desire is key in the spiritual life. We go nowhere unless we really want to get somewhere. Choose a topic (predominant desire) that is meaningful and important for you. Ask Jesus to help you realize that particular predominant desire in the coming day. If, in looking ahead at that day, you can identify a particular obstacle to the realization of your desire, ask him to help you overcome it or deal with it constructively.

The desire comes from you. The obstacles come from the situation.

For example, if my predominant desire is to live the value of "people before things," I look with particular attention during step 3 at my encounters with people during the course of the day. Did I stop what I was doing and give each one who came in to see me my full attention? Did I stop to share a personal word with colleagues in the course of the day's work? What was the quality of my interactions? Then, during step 4, I look ahead to the coming day to see what opportunities there might be to enjoy a few personal moments with people, and ask the Lord's help to keep me mindful of this desire as the events of the day unfold. If I am looking at a staff meeting as a good opportunity but see that my schedule is very tight both before and after the meeting, I have identified a particular obstacle. How can I work creatively with this to realize my desire?

In other words, your topic becomes the focus of your examen for the next day. It also determines what Jesus looks at with particular attention when you review the day with him. He is working with you for positive, concrete change by helping you take practical steps toward your deep desire.

Choosing an identifiable desire that is important to you, something you really want, is key; desire is the mainspring of growth. When using the examen with a focus on a specific topic or area, it moves it from being a general examen of consciousness to being a particular examen. When you do it, you look at everything through the filter of your predominant desire. If I do not have a topic, the examen only gives me self-knowledge. It doesn't give me Jesus as a support for my future.

Working to realize that desire in partnership with Jesus represents invaluable and effective help toward future growth. It keeps us Christ centered, living just one day at a time, and trusting in God's help to effect the transformation in us that God desires. It enables us to go forward into the future filled with hope because Jesus is going with us.

In order to discover your predominant desire, think of three or four things that you think are important for your spiritual growth. Write them down. Then imagine that you are with Jesus and have the opportunity to talk about this list of needs. Ask him if the first item you have written down is the important one for you.

When you are satisfied with his answer, then go on to ask him about the second one, and so on through your list until you are finished. Hopefully, one item will have gained ascendancy in your dialogue. That is your predominant desire, and Jesus has revealed it to you.

Once you have your topic, keep working with it on a daily basis until it is clear to you that something else is now more meaningful and needs your immediate attention. You might work with the same topic for a month, a year, or several years. The key to growth is to have a topic that is manageable and that reflects a real desire. Until another topic surfaces for you on three or four consecutive days, stay with the one you have chosen.

The examen is a particularly effective way of rededicating our lives to God each day because we literally bring the content of each day's living before Jesus, listen to and learn from his judgment, align ourselves with his wisdom, and go forward with his blessing. A convenient outline for using the examen is provided here.

Examen

1. Act of presence
Enter into dialogue with Jesus and leave behind introspective monologue.

Jesus, I want to become aware of your presence. Please be with me.
Please be patient with my "absence" from you during the day.

Make me aware of how you love me and call me to be both a friend and a disciple.

Journey with me now through my entire day and help me to see where you have been…where I missed you…

2. Petition for light, wisdom, humility

Light: that I may see clearly.

Wisdom: that I may understand what you show me.

Humility: that I may accept it and learn from it.

3. Examination with thanksgiving and/or sorrow

Look at the events and encounters of your day through Jesus' eyes, with particular attention to your predominant desire.

Let Jesus do the judging and stop the flow of your review of the day.

Where there is something for which to give thanks: "Thank you, Lord!"

Where there is something at which you experience sorrow/regret: "Forgive me, Lord!"

4. Request help for tomorrow

Focus on your predominant desire and look ahead into the next day to foresee where you are likely to need help.

End with the Lord's Prayer.

B. Meditation

One of the great graces of our time is the recovery in Christian spirituality of the earlier, rich tradition of prayer forms that are more passive in style and that dispose one to receive God's gift of contemplation. In 1974 in England the Benedictine Dom John Main opened a Christian meditation center at Ealing Abbey and three years later came to Montreal, Canada, to open a house of meditative prayer in the heart of the city that became, for a time, the motherhouse of a worldwide Christian meditation network.[2]

In 1975–76, the Trappists William Menninger, Basil Pennington, and Thomas Keating began offering retreats on what they called Centering Prayer that today also has an international network of individuals and groups through Contemplative Outreach.[3] In 1989, secular Carmelite Mary Jo Meadow with Carmelites Daniel Chowning, Kevin Culligan, and others began leading Silence and Awareness retreats through Resources for Ecumenical Spirituality.[4] All these schools of Christian prayer draw upon the same resources: classics like *The Cloud of Unknowing*, John Cassian's *Conferences*, and the writings of John of the Cross and Teresa of Avila. All are open to learning from the long meditative traditions of Eastern religions as well.

This widespread renewal in Christian forms of meditative prayer indicates the importance of becoming aware of how our subconscious energy centers of security, power, and esteem influence our behavior. Unless we find a method by which to recognize their operation and gradually disconnect them, we can continue to read books and make retreats without realizing genuine change or transformation. We must learn how to tune in to our patterns of response when these energy centers are frustrated or fulfilled, and gradually dismantle them. The human instincts for survival/security, affection/esteem, and power/control are good instincts. It is when they are frustrated through the hard knocks of life that things begin to go awry. The pain is stored and repressed in the subconscious, which then sets up ways (operations of the false self) of getting these needs met.

Meditation, coupled with mindfulness practice throughout the day, attacks the three energy centers of the false self in several ways. First, it is in the "resting in God" of meditation that the doors to the subconscious go ajar, and some of what is held in it slips through and comes to consciousness. Thus, meditation serves the critical function of exposing and bringing to awareness the false self's strategies and the wounds that necessitated their development.

Second, once we become aware of the false self's operation, we must develop a follow-up strategy to unplug it. This is where careful observance of "mindspeech" and of the movements of our hearts in daily living is of the essence. If we become skilled in seeing the emotion as it arises, and recognize the place from which it comes (the desire for security, esteem, control), there is a moment of freedom in that recognition in which we have a choice. Do we choose to act on the impulse or give it expression in words; or do we choose not to act or to speak? When we see, judge, and act, we are growing in spiritual freedom.

Third, in coming before God each day with an open and surrendered heart, we open the doors wide to God's self-communication (transforming grace).

In the context of what was articulated in chapter 1 about the Self, ego, and false self, there are several factors that recommend this prayer form. The way of conscious communion with God through transcendence of the ego is the predominant Christian pathway to the direct experience of the Self-God union. Consciousness loses its egoic form when deprived of sensory information, the desire for some particular data to work on, and the activities of the imagination and reasoning. We might say that, in such cases, the ego is deliberately deconstructed by diminishing as far as possible the operation of those faculties that make egoic life possible.

The three essential characteristics of most meditative methods of this nature are as follows:

1. Reduction of the flow of sensory information. The body may be calmed through yogic stretches; meditation proceeds in a quiet environment; the eyes are closed; a posture is assumed that minimizes body distractions.

2. Reduction of the activity of the intellect. Attention may be directed to the breath; a mantra or prayer word may be repeated continuously or when distracting thoughts emerge; one observes distractions "from a distance," without becoming involved in them.

3. Reduction of the movement of the will to a state of desiring no thing and of simple openness to God. Numbers 1 and 2 above contribute to this somewhat, but more important is the ongoing practice of nonattachment to the things and experiences of this world. If the will must be given any "goal," it is to be lovingly present to the moment, with no strings attached, ready to receive whatever God gives. Through faithfully putting oneself before God in this manner, the Holy Spirit helps us grow in this intentionality and stay rooted in it throughout the day.[5]

For those who may wish to learn more about this way of prayer in one of its forms, here are some theological and scriptural points of reference, as well as some practical "how-to" recommendations.

Christian Meditation

Meditation as a Universal Path

Meditation is the way most commonly employed by seekers of God throughout history in their quest to penetrate surface appearances and come to grips with the Real. Meditation is not intellectual effort to master certain ideas about God. Its purpose is not to acquire or to deepen our speculative knowledge of God or of revelation. Rather than seeking to know *about* God through words, thoughts, and images, the meditator is seeking to *experience God directly* with the awareness of loving faith.

Christian Faith in God's Indwelling Presence

In the Gospel of John in the New Testament, Jesus affirms God's indwelling presence. "I will ask the Father and He will give you another Advocate to be with you forever, the Spirit of truth whom…you know because he abides with you and will be in you" (14:7). And again: "Those who love me will keep my word, and my Father will love them, and we will come to them and make our home with them" (14:23). Jesus' invitation is to abide in him; his promise is that he will abide in us (15:4). Paul's letters refer to the mystery of Christ, "hidden throughout the ages," which is "Christ in you" (Col. 1:27, 28).

Accessing the Divine Presence Within

The form of prayer referred to here by the term "meditation" is based upon the conviction that, in addition to the mind and imagination with which we ordinarily communicate with God, we are endowed with what the Christian tradition calls a "mystical heart," a faculty that makes it possible for us to be aware of the Divine Presence within, to grasp and intuit God's presence and being, though in a dark manner, apart from all images and concepts that necessarily distort God's reality. In most of us, this heart lies dormant and undeveloped. If it were to be awakened, it would be constantly straining toward God.

Discerning God's Revelation in Everything

The Christian monastic tradition developed a progressive way of awakening this mystical heart and coming to an experiential awareness of God. This process was called *lectio divina*, Latin for "divine reading." Knowing a little about this process helps one see where the practice of quiet, passive prayer enters into the Christian tradition. *Lectio* is the process of discerning the ways that a word of revelation from God can come to us: through the scriptures, the words or examples of others, art, or nature. Reading a passage from scripture, for example, is like putting food whole into the mouth. This is the first step, called *lectio* or active listening/reading. One then "chews" or meditates on it, a process that takes the word from the mind into the heart; this second step is called *meditatio* or reflection. The third step comes when the heart is touched by this word of revelation and is moved, responding in gratitude, love, and prayer *(oratio)*. There is a point at which the reality of this word, and its Source, become so deeply felt that we let go of our dependency on thoughts, words, and images in responding. We simply come *to be* before the One Who Is, in full, loving attention. This final stage of the *lectio divina* process is called *contemplatio* or contemplation; it is here that the quiet, passive form of meditative prayer enters into Christian practice.

Contemplative Prayer

In contemplation, one's whole being says "Yes" to the word of revelation and to God. It is an awareness that God is not only close or present, but is intimately present within us as the source of our being. In the words of twentieth-century spiritual writer Thomas Merton, "Contemplation is a simple intuition of God, produced immediately in the soul by God and giving the soul a direct but obscure and mysterious experiential appreciation of God." Coming to this awareness of the indwelling Divine Presence is the birthright of all Christians, the natural development of the grace of baptism. It is that communion with the Divine that is the longing of our hearts.

The Method of Christian Meditation

Meditation, as we are using the word here, is not contemplation in the strict sense, because contemplative awareness is regarded as a gift of the Holy Spirit. Rather, meditation is a preparation for contemplation. It is a way of reducing the hyperactivity of our lives and bringing us to a state of quiet, open receptivity wherein we are ready to receive the grace of contemplation. Today, Christian meditation represents a recovery and renewal of the fifth-century teachings of John Cassian, the Eastern Christian practice of the "Jesus prayer," and the principles found in the fourteenth-century classic *The Cloud of Unknowing* and other sources. In the 1970s, Benedictines and Trappists began bringing the scattered elements of the tradition together, putting order in it with an eye toward our contemporary inclination for simple, clear, "how-to" instructions. What follows are the guidelines for the practice of Christian meditation in the teaching of the Benedictine Dom John Main:

The Essential Teaching

1. Seek a quiet place.

2. Sit in a comfortable, upright position, relaxed but alert with your eyes lightly closed. Remain as still as possible.

3. Silently, interiorly, begin to say a single word. We recommend the prayer word "Maranatha." Say it like this:

   MA-RA-NA-THA, in four equally stressed syllables. Some people find it helpful to say the word in conjunction with their calm and regular breathing.

4. Do not think or imagine anything, spiritual or otherwise. When thoughts and images come and your attention strays, gently return to your word.

5. Meditate each morning and evening for twenty to thirty minutes.

Commentary on the Essential Teaching

1. A *Quiet Place:* Choose a quiet corner of your room. A space that you use only for meditation and that is free from other associations is ideal. Decorate it with an icon, a candle, or an open Bible. If there is no quiet place in your home, look for one along the way of your daily route, such as a church.

2. *Posture:* Find a posture in which you can be settled, still, and alert. Be comfortable so that for the duration of the meditation period the mind will not need to tend to the body. A quiet body inclines a quiet mind. An erect but not

rigid spine facilitates easeful breathing and alert wakeful-ness. Examples: sitting in a straight-backed chair; sitting with one's seat on a prayer bench and one's knees on the floor; sitting cross-legged on the floor with the buttocks slightly elevated by a cushion.

3. *The Prayer Word: Maranatha* is Aramaic (Jesus' own lan-guage) and means "Come Lord!" It is probably the most ancient Christian prayer. St. Paul ends his first letter to the Corinthians with it, and St. John ends the Book of Revelation with it. Because it is a foreign word, people gen-erally do not have a lot of thoughts and images attached to it, which is an advantage, since meditation is a way of prayer that goes beyond thoughts and images. Other prayer words or phrases are possible, and the tradition has many of them. Whatever your sacred word, by saying it with faith and with love, one generates the flow of faith and love in one's heart. Prayer's first effect is in us.

Faithful repetition of the word is significant both in terms of *attention* and *intention*. The nature of the mind is to pro-duce thoughts. One cannot expect the mind to all of a sud-den come to a screeching halt just because it's time to meditate. So the mind is given something to occupy it: a single word, which "thins out" the flow of thoughts in the mind and holds one's attention on the Presence within. The word also carries one's intention, one's consent, to the work of God in us.

Some may say *ma-ra* on an inbreath, and *na-tha* on an outbreath. Others may find it more natural to say just one syllable on each inbreath and outbreath. While it is help-ful to say the word in the way that synchronizes with natu-ral body rhythms, if this makes it more complex, one should simply say one's word without giving any attention to this. The body has its own innate wisdom and will even-tually regulate things naturally. Other words may also be used. An appropriate prayer word or phrase summarizes one's movement to God in faith and love.

4. *Thoughts, Images, Feelings, Memories, Sense Perceptions That Engage the Mind:* All of these are a normal experi-ence in meditation. Expect a constant flow of them. To try to suppress all thoughts and feelings is both impossible and unhealthy. It is a question of not entering into dialogue with them, of not investing any energy by reacting, resist-ing, or retaining them. Just let them go. Their surfacing and passing up and out is part of the healing process of emptying, purification, and liberation that makes medita-tion a divine therapy. Each time you become aware that you have been "hooked," gently return to your word, allow-ing it to repeatedly express your intention to be before the One Who Is, in full, loving attention.

5. *Time and Frequency:* The traditional times of meditation in all the world religions are early morning and late after-noon/early evening, before meals if at all possible. The rec-ommendation of twenty to thirty minutes is made with an eye to two things: (1) the minimal amount of time gener-ally considered necessary to establish inner silence; and (2) the maximum amount of time most contemporary people can realistically afford. The end of the prayer period

can be indicated by a timer, provided it does not have a loud tick or make a startling sound when it goes off. At the end of meditation, some make a gradual transition back into cognitive activity by slowly, silently reciting a prayer expressing the attitude of openness and surrender that they have embodied during their time of prayer.

Finding Support for Your Practice

The "how-to" of meditation is simple. What is difficult is faithfulness to the discipline, holding that priority in place, interrupting what you are doing in order to pray. A support group that prays and shares together once a week helps to maintain one's commitment and provides an opportunity for further input on a regular basis through talks, tapes, and discussion.

C. Communal and Individual Prayers

The Christian life is a communal endeavor. Life in Christ is found in our interactions with others at home, at work, in our social networks, both within and without the community of faith. In the context of community, we find the risen Christ in our midst and come to realize that he lives in the weaknesses, sufferings, and energy experienced in the network of relationships within the community. An authentic Christian spirituality will keep the individual interacting, working, and praying with others in community.

The prime expression of this communal dimension of spirituality is the Eucharist. Regular participation in the Lord's Supper is vital. Word, bread, cup, and the supportive witness of other pilgrims are given to us as directions, provisions, and moral support for the journey. No traveler should ever be far from map and compass, food and drink, and the company of others. Christians also gather to faithfully listen to and reflect on the Word of God, offering intercessions and joining their voices together in song-prayers.

Individual Prayers of Dedication

There is a prayer by Ignatius of Loyola that is quite widely known and is given to the retreatant at the end of the thirty-day Spiritual Exercises: "Take, Lord, and Receive." It has even been put to music[6] and is sung regularly at eucharistic celebrations. It is not a prayer with which one *begins* either the Exercises or the Christian life; it is the kind of prayer that one "grows into," and that comes with a certain level of experience in relationship with Christ. One realizes this in witnessing the reaction of people who come to it "cold": "Are you kidding? I don't want to pray for senility and bondage!" First, the prayer, and then its context.

Take, Lord, and receive all my liberty,
my memory, my understanding, my entire will,
all that I have and possess.
You have given it all to me.
To you, Lord, I return it.
All is yours.
Dispose of it wholly according to your will.
Give me only your love and your grace,
for this is enough for me.

Knowing the context in which Ignatius proposes this prayer can open it up even for those who know it and who may have been praying it for years as a general prayer of self-offering. It is given in the final two days of the Exercises and appears in the middle of a prayer exercise entitled "Contemplation to Attain the Love of God." He prefaces it with a note: "Before presenting this exercise it will be good to call attention to two points: (1) The first is that love ought to manifest itself in deeds rather than words. (2) The second is that love consists in a mutual sharing of goods."

After reflecting on these points, one is invited "to ask for an intimate knowledge of the many blessings received, that filled with gratitude for all, I may in all things love and serve the Divine Majesty." One is then directed to systematically ponder the blessings of creation and redemption, special favors received, etc.—in short, how much God has done for me, how much God has shared with me.

For anyone really interested in getting "inside" this prayer and coming to a deeper appreciation of the "heart space" from which it arises, I would suggest going to a park, preferably, one with a lake or a river. Take along something tasty to eat. Once you've arrived, find a spot by a tree near the water and just sit down. Begin to look carefully at what is around you: grass, plants, trees, flowers, earth, rocks, insects, water, animals, birds.

After an unrushed, general, appreciative look, isolate and concentrate on each one of your senses. Get up and move around to rub your hand over the tree bark, the rocks, the dirt, the grass; to rub a leaf between your fingers, to pet a dog. Then find whatever you can to smell. After that, close your eyes and listen to the sound of the water and wind, birdsong, human voices. Then take out what you brought along to eat—a peach, a tangerine—and bite into it like you've never tasted one of these before. Finally, lay back and feel the warmth of the sun on your skin.

While looking again at all the created wonders around you, reflect along these lines: "God, you've given *all this* to me! What do I have to offer to you…?" I know it's silly to put a monetary value on creation, but just for the sake of the exercise, what do you think all that you behold is worth? Fifty billion? A trillion? Again, knowing that love ought to manifest itself in deeds, and consists in a mutual sharing of goods, what do you have to offer in return?

This is the "heart space" of gratitude out of which the prayer comes. Get inside it and have your own experience with it. My "dialogue" with it, given here in italics between the lines of the prayer itself, sounds something like this:

Take, Lord, and receive all my liberty,
To do your will is my choice, for in it I find true freedom
my memory,
which holds your saving acts and your promises of future ful-
    fillment;
my understanding,
which is always seeking after your truth;
my entire will,
which enables me to love, to will the good of another.
all that I have and possess.
These three faculties of my soul are my most precious posses-
    sions, eternally outlasting my health or anything material
    that I own; by offering you the best, I offer you all
You have given all to me,

*life, faith, family, education, health, friends, spouse, chil-
dren, the earth and its creatures.*

To you, Lord, I return it.

(All that you have given to me personally), because

All is yours.

Nothing is "mine"; I only hold all things in trust.

Dispose of it wholly according to your will.

*Invest the little offering I have to make wherever you wish.
You can do a lot with a little.*

Give me your love and your grace, for this is enough for
me.

*I know that if you are the foundation of my life, all shall be
well.*

*Other Prayers for Dedicating
One's Life to God Each Day*

Here is a selection of other prayers of self-offering and dedication for your use. If there is one that appeals to you, make a copy
and place it where you will see it each morning upon rising. Or
use a different prayer for each day of the week as a way of keeping the sentiments fresh through the use of different words.

✒

Take my life and let it be
Consecrated, God, to thee;
Take my moments and my days,
Let them flow in ceaseless praise.
Take my hands and let them move

At the impulse of thy love;
Take my feet, and let them be,
Swift and beautiful for thee.
Take my lips, and let them be
Filled with messages from Thee.
Take my silver and my gold,
Not a mite would I withhold;
Take my intellect and use
Every power as thou shalt choose.
Take my will, and make it thine,
It shall be no longer mine;
Take my heart, it is thine own;
It shall be thy royal throne.
Take my love; my God, I pour
At thy feet its treasure store;
Take myself, and I will be,
Ever, only, all, for thee. Amen.
(Frances Ridley Havergal, abridged)

🌿

Loving God, I abandon myself into your hands.
Do with me what you will.
Whatever you may do, I thank you.
Help me to be ready for all, to accept all.
Let only your will be done in me and in all your creatures.
I ask no more than this.
Father, into your hands I commend my life.
I give it to you with all the love of my heart,
for I love you

and so need to give myself to you,
to surrender myself into your hands
without reserve and with complete confidence
for you are my Father.
(Charles de Foucauld, the founder of the Little Brothers and
Sisters of Jesus)

✒

Loving and tender providence of my God,
into your hands I commend my spirit;
to you I abandon my hopes and fears,
my desires and repugnancies,
my temporal and eternal prospects.

To you I commit the wants of my perishable body;
to you I commit the more precious interests
of my immortal soul
for whose lot I have nothing to fear
so long as I do not leave your care.

Though my faults are many,
my spiritual poverty evident,
my hope in you surpasses all.
It is superior to my weakness,
greater than my difficulties,
stronger than death.

Though temptations should assail me,
I will hope in you;
though I break my resolutions,

I will look to you confidently for grace to keep them at last.
Though you should ask me to die,
even then I will trust you,
for you are my God,
the support of my salvation.

You are my kind, compassionate, indulgent parent,
and I am your devoted son/daughter.
I cast myself into your arms and beg your blessings.
I put my trust in you,
and so trusting, shall not be confounded.
Amen.[7]
(Claude La Columbière, S.J.)

🖋

In stillness
And silence
I know
You are my God
And I love you
silence
There is no
Felt awareness
But deeper inside
Than I knew existed
I am with you
silence
All else
is of no account
My pride, self-doubt

Inhibitions
Washed aside
silence
Held in being
Loved into life
Delicately balanced
Joy transcending
Aching anguish
silence
Called by name
Compelled by Love
Desiring nothing
Except your will
Expressed in me[8]
(Christine Bull)

I am giving You worship with my whole life,
I am giving You assent with my whole power,
I am giving You praise with my whole tongue,
I am giving You honor with my whole utterance.
I am giving you love with my whole devotion,
I am giving you love kneeling with my whole desire,
I am giving you love with my whole heart,
I am giving you affection with my whole sense,
I am giving You my existence with my whole mind,
I am giving you my soul, O God of all gods.[9]
(Esther de Vaal)

Dear God,
I surrender to You my doings this day.
I ask only that they serve You and the healing of the world.
May I bring Your love and goodness with me, to give
unto others wherever I go.
Make me the person You would have me be.
Direct my footsteps, and show me what You would have me
  do.
Make the world a safer, more beautiful place.
Bless all your creatures.
Heal us all, and use me, Dear Lord, that I might know the
  joy
of being used by You.[10]
(Marianne Williamson)

🌿

Gladly do I give my life to Thee,
Not solemnly, not grudgingly,
But I would take my life and fling
It at Thy feet—and sing and sing—
Happy to bring Thee this small thing.[11]
(Mary Dixon Thayer)

🌿

O Heart of love, I place my trust in you.
Although I fear all things from my weakness,
I hope all things from your goodness.[12]
(St. Margaret-Mary Alacoque)

All I have is Yours, do what seems best according to Your divine will. Let not the cares or duties of this life press on me too heavily; but lighten my burden, that I may follow Your way in quietness, filled with thankfulness for Your mercy, and rendering acceptable service unto You.[13]

(Maria Hare)

🌿

Jesus, may all that is you flow into me.
May your body and blood
be my food and drink.
May your passion and death
be my strength and life.
Jesus, with you by my side
enough has been given.
May the shelter I seek
be the shadow of your cross.
Let me not run from the love
which you offer,
But hold me safe from the forces of evil.
On each of my dyings
shed your light and your love.
Keep calling to me until that day comes,
When, with your saints,
I may praise you forever. Amen.[14]

(David L. Fleming, S.J.)

🌿

Closing Words

I can think of no more appropriate parting words to offer you for the journey to spiritual freedom than these, for the main thing is to keep the love growing and deepening.

Nothing is more practical than finding God,
that is, than falling in love
in a quite absolute, final way.
What you are in love with,
what seizes your imagination,
will affect everything.
It will decide what will get you
out of bed in the morning,
what you will do with your evenings,
how you will spend your weekends,
what you read, who you know,
what breaks your heart,
and what amazes you with joy and gratitude.
Fall in love; stay in love,
and it will decide everything.[15]

Reflection Questions

A. What checks and supports in your life help you keep first things first?

B. What "freedom tools" are you already using?

C. What additional ways of daily rededicating your life to God would work best for you?

Notes

Chapter 1

1. The Spiritual Exercises written by Ignatius are generally laid out over thirty days. Some retreat centers today, however, are offering a forty-day model with five days of preparation preceding the actual Exercises themselves and ending with five days of integration. The thirty-day retreat calls for retreatants to spend five hours a day in prayer and is divided into four blocks of time that are approximately one week each. The nineteenth annotation of the Exercises—so labeled by Ignatius when he wrote them—is an at-home retreat that consists of an eight-month program of prayer in which those doing the Exercises commit to an hour a day of prayer following the pattern of scripture reading, prayer, and contemplation as indicated by Ignatius. The nineteenth-annotation version follows the liturgical calendar where possible, beginning in the autumn and ending around Easter. The nineteenth-annotation version of the Spiritual Exercises is also available on-line, though without benefit of a spiritual director: www.creighton.edu/CollaborativeMinistry/online.html. Father Joseph Tetlow, S.J., wrote in *National Jesuit News* in 1995 that "It would be safe to say that more people are engaged in these exercises today than at any time in history."

2. John J. English, S.J., *Spiritual Freedom* (Chicago: Loyola Press, 1995), 18, 20, 21, 36. There is some difference of opinion about the purpose of the Spiritual Exercises. In the view of most commentators, the purpose is for the one making the Exercises to arrive at some kind of a decision. But others suggest that the Exercises are meant to be a school of prayer or an instrument for bringing one into union with God. These two expressions of the purpose may well come to the same thing. A reliable decision demands closer union with God; and the closer one draws to God, the more often God demands decisions in response. In either case, a person needs to become free. The Exercises are an instrument for helping a person come to that spiritual freedom.

3. In a 1998 audiotaped presentation entitled *On Being and Doing* at the Kripalu Center for Yoga and Health, Stephen Cope (crediting Deepak Chopra with naming these four themes) worked with them as "four pillars" in the Bhagavad Gita. The variety of contexts in which these themes appear, such as in the Gita and in Ignatian spirituality based on the Exercises, demonstrates their universality in the spiritual life. I am indebted to Cope and Chopra for naming these archetypal themes in a way that makes them more intelligible to modern ears.

4. John V. Taylor, *A Matter of Life and Death* (London: SCM Press, 1986), 41.

5. See also Luke 8:19–21; Luke 2:48–50; John 2:4.

6. Taylor, 42, 43.

7. Wilkie Au, *By Way of the Heart* (Mahwah, N.J.: Paulist Press, 1989), 118, 119.

8. Taylor, 40.

9. Au, 123.

10. Thomas Dubay, *Fire Within* (San Francisco: Ignatius Press, 1989), 132.

11. Ibid., 135, 146.

12. Ibid., 144, 146.

13. Anthony de Mello, *The Heart of the Enlightened* (New York: Doubleday, 1989), 30, 31.

14. Jean Vanier, *Becoming Human* (Mahwah, N.J.: Paulist Press, 1999) 108, 109.

15. Dan Danielson, "What Does True Freedom Really Mean?" in *Prairie Messenger*, June 20, 2001, 12.

16. Ibid.

17. Vanier, 124.

Chapter 2

1. See, for example, Walter E. Conn, *The Desiring Self* (Mahwah, N.J.: Paulist Press, 1998); *Self and Liberation: The Jung/Buddhist Dialogue,* Daniel J. Meckel and Robert L. Moore, eds. (Mahwah, N.J.: Paulist Press, 1992).

2. See Anne E. Carr's *A Search for Wisdom and Spirit: Thomas Merton's Theology of the Self* (Notre Dame, Ind.: University of Notre Dame Press, 1988).

3. Thomas Merton, *Seeds of Contemplation* (New York: Dell, 1960 [1949]), 20, 22.

4. Ibid., 41, 40, 23.

5. Thomas Merton, *New Seeds of Contemplation,* (New York: New Directions, 1972 [1961]), 7, 38.

6. Wilkie Au, *By Way of the Heart* (Mahwah, N.J.: Paulist Press, 1989), 121.

7. Johannes B. Metz, *Poverty of Spirit* (New York: Paulist Press, 1968), 44, 45.

8. Paul Ricoeur, *Symbolism of Evil* (Boston: Beacon Press, 1967), 52.

9. Howard Gray, S.J., in an address at Clarkston, Michigan, June 15, 1985.

10. Walter Grundman, "Sin in the New Testament," in *Theological Dictionary of the New Testament I,* ed. Gerhard Kittel (Grand Rapids, Mich.: Eerdmans, 1964), 303.

11. John Renard, *Responses to 101 Questions on Buddhism* (Mahwah, N.J.: Paulist Press, 1999), 71.

12. John Renard, *Responses to 101 Questions on Hinduism* (Mahwah, N.J.: Paulist Press, 1999), 60, 61.

13. R. Reitzenstein and G. Kittel, as cited by Grundman, "Sin in the New Testament," op.cit., 308 ff.

14. Ibid., 308.

15. William Rusch, "How the Eastern Fathers Understood What the Western Church Meant by Justification," in *Justification by Faith*, ed. H. George Anderson, T. Austin Murphy, and Joseph A. Burgess (Minneapolis: Augsburg, 1985), 132.

16. Valerie Karras, "Beyond Justification: An Orthodox Perspective," a presentation given at the North American Academy of Ecumenists meeting in St. Louis, Mo., on October 1, 2000. Dr. Karras's further exposition: "The concept of original guilt was developed in the early fifth century primarily by Augustine, who reacted to Pelagius's claim that infants need not be baptized since they have committed no personal sins. Augustine countered Pelagius by arguing from the common Church practice of baptizing infants and mixing it with Romans 5:12: '…sin came into the world through one man and death came through sin, and so death spread to all because all have sinned.' To briefly summarize Augustine's argument…: the Church universally baptized infants; therefore, since baptism confers remission of sins, and since infants have committed no personal sins, the Church baptizes infants obviously in order to remit the original sin which they receive hereditarily from Adam because all of humanity was seminally present in Adam."

17. Ibid. There are interesting echoes in this understanding, to be further explored in interreligious dialogue, with the Buddhist understanding of the abuse of human freedom as ignorance, and in the Upanishads, of sin as a failure of knowledge.

18. Ibid.

19. Ibid.

20. J. Philip Newell, *Echo of the Soul* (Harrisburg, Pa.: Morehouse, 2000), 60.

21. Au, 195.

22. David M. Thorpe, *Share the Word* (September-November, 1999), 34.

23. Newell, *Echo of the Soul*, xiv.

24. John Meyendorff, "Humanity: 'Old' and 'New'—Anthropological Considerations," in *Salvation in Christ: A Lutheran-Orthodox Dialogue*, ed. John Meyendorff and Robert Tobias (Minneapolis: Augsburg, 1992), 63.

25. Valerie Karras, "Beyond Justification: An Orthodox Perspective," op. cit.

26. As quoted in Newell, op. cit., 7, 8.

27. Ibid., 14.

Chapter 3

1. Conn, *The Desiring Self*, 5.

2. Philip St. Romain, *Handbook for Spiritual Growth* (Liguori, Mo.: Liguori, 1993), 23–25.

3. Thomas Merton, *New Seeds of Contemplation*, 7.

4. Thomas Keating has given extensive development to the false self's emotional programs for happiness in the video series *A Spiritual Journey: A Contemporary Presentation of Christian Growth and Transformation* and its attendant handbook, *The Spiritual Journey* (Colorado Springs, Colo.: Contemporary Communications, 1989 [1987]), as well as in his book *Invitation to Love* (New York: Continuum, 1996).

5. Stephen Cope, *Yoga and the Quest for the True Self* (New York: Bantam, 1999), 93.

6. Vanier, *Becoming Human*, 114, 117.

7. Cope, op. cit., 129.

8. For a fuller development, see St. Romain, *Handbook for Spiritual Growth*, 27–36.

9. Merton, *New Seeds of Contemplation*, 34, 35.

10. Vanier, *Becoming Human*, 121.

Chapter 4

1. Thomas Merton, *Contemplative Prayer* (New York: Image Books, Doubleday, 1971), 34.

2. Thomas Merton, *A Thomas Merton Reader*, ed. Thomas P. McDonnell (New York: Image Books, Doubleday, 1974), 515.

3. James Finley, *Merton's Palace of Nowhere* (Notre Dame, Ind.: Ave Maria Press, 1978), 125.

4. As quoted by Brian Swimme, in Canticle to the Cosmos videotape series, tape 4, *The Fundamental Order of the Universe*.

5. Ibid.

6. Thomas Merton, "The Contemplative Life: Its Meaning and Necessity," *Dublin Review*, CCXXII (1949), 28.

7. Merton, *New Seeds of Contemplation*, 36.

8. Karlfried Graf Dürckheim, *L'Expérience de la Transcendence* (Paris: Albin Michel, 1984), 38.

9. Philip St. Romain, "God, Self, and Ego," unpublished paper (December 1995), 20, 21.

10. Beatrice Bruteau, *What Can We Learn from the East?* (New York: Crossroad, 1995), 67.

11. Thomas Keating, *Invitation to Love* (New York: Continuum, 1997), 10.

12. Ibid., 34.

Chapter 5

1. Elizabeth-Anne Vanek, *From Center to Circumference: God's Place in the Circle of Self* (Mahwah, N.J.: Paulist Press, 1996), 42.

2. Ibid, 8.

3. Ibid., 24.

4. Ibid., 28, 29, 30.

5. Meister Eckhart, Sermon 1, in *Meister Eckhart: A Modern Translation*, trans. and ed. Raymond Bernard Blakney (New York: Harper & Row, 1941), 97.

6. Kerry Walters, *Practicing Presence: The Spirituality of Caring in Everyday Life* (Franklin, Wis.: Sheed & Ward, 2001), 48.

7. Eckhart, 163.

8. Walters, 49, 50.

9. Ibid., 51–53.

Chapter 6

1. Julia Cameron, *The Artist's Way: A Spiritual Path to Higher Creativity* (New York: Jeremy P. Tarcher/Putnam, 1992), 108.

2. Thomas Merton, *Spiritual Direction and Meditation* (Collegeville, Minn.: Liturgical Press), 31.

3. Wilkie Au, *By Way of the Heart: Toward a Holistic Christian Spirituality* (Mahwah, N.J.: Paulist Press, 1989), 73.

4. Ibid., 74, 75.

5. *Call to Commitment* (New York: Harper and Row, 1963) and *Journey Inward and Journey Outward* (New York: Harper and Row, 1968), both by Elizabeth O'Connor.

6. David Lonsdale, *Eyes to See, Ears to Hear: An Introduction to Ignatian Spirituality* (Maryknoll, N.Y.: Orbis), 89, 91.

7. Ibid., 91.

8. Ibid., 92.

9. Ibid.

10. Ron Delbene and Herb Montgomery, *The Breath of Life* (Minneapolis, Minn.: Winston Press, 1981), 8, 9.

11. Anthony de Mello, *One Minute Wisdom* (New York: Doubleday, 1988), 68.

12. E. Edward Kinerk, "Eliciting Great Desires: Their Place in the Spirituality of the Society of Jesus," *Studies in the Spirituality of Jesuits*, XVI:5 (Nov. 1984), 2.

13. As quoted in *Words to Live By*, Eknath Easwaren, ed. (Petaluma, Calif.: Nilgiri Press, 1990), 68.

14. Cameron, *Artist's Way*, 195.

15. M. Scott Peck, *A World Waiting to Be Born* (New York: Bantam, 1993), 9.

16. Lonsdale, *Eyes to See, Ears to Hear*, 90.

17. Cameron, *Artist's Way*, 92.

Chapter 7

1. William A. Barry, S.J., *Allowing the Creator to Deal with the Creature: An Approach to the Spiritual Exercises of Ignatius of Loyola* (Mahwah, N.J.: Paulist Press, 1994), 72, 74.

2. Au, *By Way of the Heart*, 77.

3. Ibid., 76.

4. John Govan, Spiritual Exercises Institute notes, Guelph, Ontario, October 1–November 10, 1999.

5. Au, 77.

6. Ibid., 78, 79

7. Ibid., 80.

8. Walter Brueggemann, *Living Toward a Vision* (Philadelphia: United Church Press, 1976), 15, 16.

9. Barry, *Allowing the Creator*, 77, 78.

10. Václav Havel, *Living in Truth* (London and Boston: Faber & Faber, 1989), 153, 154.

11. As quoted in Dan Wakefield, *Returning: A Spiritual Journey* (New York: Penguin Books, 1984), 26.

12. William A. Barry, S.J., *Spiritual Direction and the Encounter with God: A Theological Inquiry* (Mahwah, N.J.: Paulist Press, 1992), 78.

Chapter 8

1. Thomas Ryan, *Disciplines for Christian Living: Interfaith Perspectives* (Mahwah, N.J.: Paulist Press, 1994) and *Prayer of Heart and Body: Meditation and Yoga as Christian Spiritual Practice* (Mahwah, N.J.: Paulist, 1995).

2. Jacqueline McMakin and Rhoda Nary, *Discovering Your Gifts, Vision, and Call* (HarperSanFrancisco: 1993).

3. Barry, *Allowing the Creator*, 97, 98, 101.

Chapter 9

1. Unitas spent about two years in this new location, and then moved again, dropping its residential component and trimming its programmatic offerings. Its priority is the promotion of Christian meditation and related activities such as *Lectio Divina*, Twilight Retreats, Taizé prayer

evenings, and Prayer of Heart and Body (yoga and meditation) sessions. Website address: www.unitasmeditation.ca.

Chapter 10

1. Eknath Easwaran, in his introduction to *The Bhagavad Gita*, Eknath Easwaran, trans. (Tomales, Calif.: Nilgiri Press, 1985), 1. Addressed to everyone, of whatever background or status, the Gita distills the loftiest truths of India's ancient wisdom into simple, memorable poetry that haunts the mind and informs the affairs of everyday life. Its literary context is the *Mahabharata*, a vast epic comparable in its breadth and characterization to the *Iliad* and the *Odyssey* or to Shakespeare. Every Hindu child is raised on the imagery and stories of the family intrigues and great battles of the *Mahabharata*. Within this epic stands the Gita, like a jewel in a crown, as a timeless, practical manual for daily living.

2. Ibid., 4, 5. The study and reflection leading to these conclusions was considered the supreme science because it sought knowledge of any underlying reality that would inform all other studies and activities. The discoveries of this supreme science *(bramavidya)* were committed to writing in the Upanishads, visionary documents that are the earliest and purest statement of the Perennial Philosophy. To the mind of some, the Bhagavad Gita (The Song of the Lord) is an Upanishad, a mystical statement incorporated into the warrior epic *Mahabharata* at a later age.

3. Ibid., 32, 33.

4. Ibid., 33, 34.

5. As quoted in the introduction to *The Bhagavad Gita*, Easwaran, trans., 35.

6. Ibid.

7. John of the Cross, *Ascent of Mount Carmel*, book 1, ch. 11: 4.

8. Johannes B. Metz, *Poverty of Spirit* (New York: Paulist Press, 1968), 18, 19.

Chapter 11

1. John Kabat-Zinn, *Full Catastrophe Living* (New York: Dell, 1990), 4, 5.

2. Ibid., 6

3. Judith Viorst, *Necessary Losses: The Loves, Illusions, Dependencies, and Impossible Expectations That All of Us Have to Give Up in Order to Grow* (New York: Ballantine Books, 1986), 3.

4. Faith Nostbakken, excerpted from a fuller presentation entitled "Stories of Faith and Hope," at the Health and Wellness Seminar at Mount Olivet Lutheran Church, Sherwood Park Alberta, Feb. 24, 2001. Used with permission.

5. Brian Swimme, *Canticle to the Cosmos,* 12-tape video series, tape 5: *Loss and Destruction.*

6. Ibid., tape 7:1, *Sex, Death, and Dreams.*

7. Kathleen Norris, *Amazing Grace: A Vocabulary of Faith* (New York: Riverhead Books, 1998), 110.

8. Elizabeth-Anne Vanek, *From Center to Circumference,* 18.

9. John V. Taylor, *A Matter of Life and Death,* 63.

Chapter 12

1. The phrase "secondhand religion" comes from William James, *The Varieties of Religious Experience,* ed. Martin Marty (New York: Penguin, 1982 [1902]), 6.

2. Marcus J. Borg, *Meeting Jesus Again for the First Time* (New York: HarperCollins, 1994), 87.

3. Ibid., 88.

4. See Thomas Ryan, *Disciplines for Christian Living* (Mahwah, N.J.: Paulist Press, 2001 [1994]), 22–24, 257–59.

5. Parker J. Palmer, *The Promise of Paradise* (Notre Dame, Ind.: Ave Maria Press, 1980), 109.

6. Letter to Dom Bede Griffiths, O.S.B., April 23, 1951, in *Letters of C. S. Lewis*, ed. Walter Hooper (New York: Harcourt Brace, 1994), 228.

7. Au, *By Way of the Heart*, 80, 81.

8. Jack Kornfield, *After the Ecstasy, the Laundry: How the Heart Grows Wise on the Spiritual Path* (New York: Bantam Books, 2000), 116–18.

9. Ibid., 193, 202.

Chapter 13

1. Joan Chittister, "Life Is the Best Spiritual Director," in *National Catholic Reporter*, March 9, 2001, p. 14.

2. Marion Woodman, as quoted in Wilkie Au and Noreen Cannon, "The Plague of Perfectionism," *Human Development*, 13:3 (fall 1992), 7, 8.

3. Wilkie Au and Noreen Cannon, "The Plague of Perfectionism," *Human Development*, 13:3 (fall 1992), 10, 11.

4. See footnote 5, chapter 6.

5. See www.centerforsharing.org.

Chapter 14

1. Nelson Mandela, *The Long Walk to Freedom* (Boston: Little & Brown, 1994), 363, 425.

2. Ibid., 322.

3. Gerald May, *The Awakened Heart* (New York: HarperCollins, 1991), 3, 4.

4. Ibid., 8.

5. Ibid., 9, 10.

6. As quoted in John Kirvan, *God Hunger—Discovering the Mystic in All of Us* (Notre Dame, Ind.: Sorin Books, 1999), 74.

7. May, 26, 27.

8. Ibid., 48, 49, 55.

9. Ibid., 58.

10. Ibid., 65.

11. Brother Lawrence of the Resurrection, *The Practice of the Presence of God*, John J. Delaney, trans. (New York: Doubleday, 1977).

12. May, 111.

13. Ibid., 143–45.

14. Ibid., 151.

15. Ibid., 233, 234.

Chapter 15

1. What follows is a condensed version of a booklet by John Govan, S.J., entitled *The Examen: Living and Growing with Christ* (Loyola House, Guelph, Ontario), which itself is an adaptation of his article "The Examen: A Tool for Holistic Growth," *Review for Religious*, vol. 45, no. 3 (1986), 394–401.

2. World Community of Christian Meditation International Centre, 23 Kensington Square, London W8 5HN England.
Tel: (44) 20 7937-4679. Fax: (44) 20 7937-6790 Web site: www.wccm.org.

3. Contemplative Outreach, LTD, P.O. Box 737, 10 Park Place, Suite B, Butler, N.J., 07405, U.S.A.
Tel: 973-838-3384. Fax: 973-492-5795. E-mail: office@coutreach.org. Web site: www.contemplativeoutreach.org.

4. Resources for Ecumenical Spirituality, 3407 Highway 13, Dunnegan, Mo. 65640-9620.

Tel: 417-754-2562. E-mail: resecum@juno.com.

5. Philip St. Romain, "God, Self, and Ego: An Exercise in Discernment," unpublished paper, (December 1995), 30.

6. "Take, Lord, Receive," on the CD *Let Heaven Rejoice* by the St. Louis Jesuits (Oregon Catholic Press Publications, 1997).

7. Claude La Colombière, S.J., in *Hearts on Fire: Praying with Jesuits*, Michael Harter, S.J., ed. (St. Louis: The Institute of Jesuit Sources, 1993), 68.

8. Christine Bull, in *The Flowering of the Soul: A Book of Prayers by Women*, Lucinda Vardley, ed. (Toronto: Alfred A. Knopf, 1999), 300, 301.

9. Esther de Vaal, ibid., 126

10. Marianne Williamson, ibid., 298.

11. Mary Dixon Thayer, ibid., 131.

12. St. Margaret-Mary Alacoque, ibid., 129.

13. Maria Hare, ibid., 125.

14. David L. Fleming, S.J., in *Hearts on Fire*, Michael Harter, S.J., ed. (St. Louis: The Institute of Jesuit Sources, 1993), 7.

15. Pedro Arrupe, S.J., former superior general of the Society of Jesus.